Praise for *Unshakable Leadership*

"*Unshakable Leadership* is packed with insights and reminders of what matters most in school leadership. I love its plainspoken focus on the need to define, demonstrate, monitor, and reinforce specific, high-leverage practices—to 'automaticity.' If you act on its recommendations, you *will* achieve swift, significant improvements in teaching and student outcomes."

—**Mike Schmoker**, author, speaker, consultant, and author of *Focus: Elevating the Essentials to Radically Improve Student Learning,* 3rd Edition

"Sonbert and Vance distill the essentials of impactful school leadership with rare precision. Drawing on nearly two decades across every level of urban education—from classroom paraprofessional to principal supervisor—I can attest that every insight is hard-won truth. The chapter on calendaring is a master class in reclaiming a leader's most scarce and irreplaceable resource: time."

—**Donald B. Reynolds**, Principal Supervisor, Denver Public Schools

"*Unshakable Leadership* captures what it truly takes to deliver results for scholars. It challenges leaders to hold the line on expectations and build intentional culture with clarity and courage."

—**Alfred Keith IV**, CEO, Milwaukee College Prep

"*Unshakable Leadership* offers the what, why, and how of purposeful school leadership. From vision to practice and communication to accountability, it guides leaders through the essential elements of leading with clarity and meaning. Distilling rigorous thinking into actionable insight, this book is a refreshing approach, empowering school leaders to move from understanding to effective practice—every school leader should have a copy!"

—**Kristen Foster**, Chief Education Officer, Seton Catholic Schools

“Sonbert and Vance don’t pull any punches and expose the extent of the crisis facing urban education. By providing fresh, practical wisdom, this book will help bold education leaders build the resilient schools that our kids deserve.”

—**Jorge Elorza**, CEO, Democrats for Education Reform

“This book is refreshing because it helps us understand what any school can be—and must be—in a no-nonsense way. Their strategies are borne out of experience on the ground in some challenging environments. I’ve been privileged to work with and see both Michael and Antonio make this difference. This is a toolkit to read and revisit.”

—**John Baumber**, Visiting Professor,
Sunderland and Manav Rachna Universities

UNSHAKABLE LEADERSHIP

UNSHAKABLE LEADERSHIP

21 Strategies for Success in Urban Schools and Beyond

MICHAEL SONBERT
& M. ANTONIO VANCE

Arlington, Virginia USA

iste+ascd
2111 Wilson Boulevard, Suite 300 • Arlington, VA 22201 USA
Phone: 800-933-2723 or 703-578-9600
Website: iste-ascd.org • Email: memsupport@iste-ascd.org
Author guidelines: ascd.org/write

Richard Culatta, *Chief Executive Officer;* Genny Ostertag, *Managing Director, Book Acquisitions & Editing;* Bill Varner, *Senior Acquisitions Editor;* Mary Beth Nielsen, *Director, Book Editing & Design;* Liz Wegner, *Senior Editor;* Masie Chong, *Graphic Designer;* Valerie Younkin, *Senior Production Designer;* Cynthia Stock, *Typesetter;* Emily Reed, *Senior Director, Publishing Operations*; Kelly Marshall, *Production Manager;* Shajuan Martin, *E-Publishing Specialist*

PAPERBACK ISBN: 978-1-4166-3450-8 Product #125067 n6/26

PDF EBOOK ISBN: 978-1-4166-3451-5; see Books in Print for other formats.

Quantity discounts are available: email programteam@ascd.org or call 800-933-2723, ext. 5773, or 703-575-5773. For desk copies, go to ascd.org/deskcopy.

Library of Congress Cataloging-in-Publication Data

Names: Sonbert, Michael Cary author | Vance, M. Antonio author
Title: Unshakable leadership : 21 strategies for success in urban schools and beyond / Michael Sonbert and M. Antonio Vance.
Description: Arlington, VA, USA : ISTE+ASCD, [2026] | Includes bibliographical references and index.
Identifiers: LCCN 2026011121 (print) | LCCN 2026011122 (ebook) | ISBN 9781416634508 paperback | ISBN 9781416634515 pdf | ISBN 9781416634522 epub
Subjects: LCSH: School management and organization | Educational leadership
Classification: LCC LB2805 .S7256 2026 (print) | LCC LB2805 (ebook)
LC record available at https://lccn.loc.gov/2026011121
LC ebook record available at https://lccn.loc.gov/2026011122

35 34 33 32 31 30 29 28 27 26 1 2 3 4 5 6 7 8 9 10 11 12

This book is dedicated to every single one of the thousands of school leaders, teachers, support staff, and beyond who've allowed us access to their buildings, who've shared their vulnerabilities, who've allowed us to push them, and who ultimately and unwaveringly showed up and still show up for students and families every day. We are in awe of you. Thank you.

UNSHAKABLE LEADERSHIP

Introduction

If urban education were a person, that person would be standing in the lobby of a hospital emergency room with a knife in their chest, bleeding out on the floor, while nurses and doctors—in this case, the "experts"—walked around discussing the hangnail on the patient's left pinky, an ingrown hair on their cheek, and a suspicious mole on their left calf.

That's exactly what's happening in schools in cities across the United States—nothing short of a full-scale, life-or-death emergency. But so much of what education experts write from the comfort of their offices, so far removed from schools themselves, doesn't reflect the direness of the situation. So much of the training that educators receive doesn't reflect the reality of working in a school where things need to be better for students and staff, immediately, either.

Although we planned to write this book for the educators we see as the most neglected in the country—those leading in cities—we also have countless examples of leaders who don't work in cities in the sense you or we may think of a city. Some of the leaders are in the suburbs or entirely rural areas. But what these leaders share is a willingness to be better than they were before. A willingness to ruffle feathers for the good of students. A willingness to say the tough things that need to be said, to hold adults accountable, and to be unstoppable for students. So while the book is intended for our urban partners, please know that if you're a leader like the ones we just described, or if you *hope* to be one day, this book is also for you.

As educators, we're inundated with articles and professional development from various "authorities" about new curricula, standards alignment, student trauma, implicit bias, restorative justice, social-emotional learning, cognitive coaching, and so on. At the same time, undertrained, undersupported, and often ineffective school leaders are leaving undertrained, undersupported, and often ineffective school leaders and teachers to figure school out for themselves. The result? Our most vulnerable students lose days, weeks, months, and sometimes years of learning because of bad leadership and poor teaching.

This is a tragedy. It's perpetuated by colleges that aren't adequately preparing leaders or teachers for the role of working in urban schools, by books that traffic in philosophical ideas as opposed to practical strategies for improvement, and by pundits who seem more intent on placating adults than ensuring positive change for kids. It comes down to an unwillingness to name the thing that we are willing to name right here and now: that many school leaders and teachers just aren't good enough.

But hold on a minute. Before you toss this book in the trash, we'd like to quickly add that it's likely not your fault. Most leaders are managed by district or central office personnel who don't develop them, who simply check in with them to make sure their buildings aren't burning down. Those school leaders, in turn, usually operate in the same way with other leaders on their team. They don't coach them, they don't provide ongoing feedback, and they struggle to hold them accountable.

A school leader recently told us that his leadership team had listed a half-dozen reasons for why their school was failing, which included the need for new curricula, for students to do their homework, and even for a new, more modern building. "You want to know what our biggest issue *really* is?" he noted. "Our staff is supposed to be here at 7:30 a.m. But if you looked at our empty parking lot then, you'd never know it. And no one in this room, including me, holds them accountable for getting here on time."

These leadership teams typically don't do much in terms of developing their teachers, either. If coaching happens, and it rarely does, it's often exploratory, with well-meaning leaders and coaches asking questions of and sharing resources with teachers during time-consuming meetings that don't drive change, when all the teachers really want are practical strategies for improving their teaching. We're talking about teachers who are burning out, breaking down, and leaving the profession because they don't see a light at the end of the tunnel. What these teachers want is intentional, targeted training.

Yes, student trauma is real, the teacher shortage is hurting the profession, and some schools are in neighborhoods so rife with violence that it can feel impossible to bring about change. Yes, many students in our cities have undiagnosed disabilities and disorders that make it hard for them to learn or even sit still. And yes, systems of oppression exist and have been allowed to exist for far too long.

Years ago, during a visit to a new partner school in North Philadelphia (also known as "the badlands"), we noticed something. Despite the fact that it hadn't snowed in days and that the rest of the city's streets were free of snow, the streets in North Philly were piled with ice and dirty snow. That's just another way of saying, "No one cares about this place."

We bet educators all over the United States feel like that sometimes, that no one really cares and that no one really understands. Especially when some "authority" who has never taught, led, or even been inside a school on the south side of Chicago or the north side of Milwaukee has grand ideas about how city schools need to be run. Coaching from the experts about such schools can sound impossibly out of touch.

Grounded in Reality

Together, we've spent a combined 30 years working in schools in U.S. cities. That means 30 years of teaching, coaching, leading, training, and helping to turn around struggling schools in places that most people would go out of their way to avoid.

Our team at Skyrocket Education has worked in district, charter, and faith-based schools in cities like Detroit; Chicago; Philadelphia; Milwaukee; Baltimore; Memphis; New Orleans; Dallas; Los Angeles; Cincinnati, Ohio; Akron, Ohio; Camden, New Jersey; Wilmington, Delaware; Bridgeport, Connecticut; New York City, and beyond. Although each of those cities is unique, each with its own culture, traditions, and beliefs, all rife with passionate educators and exceptional children, the challenges *are* strikingly similar.

No, not every student who attends schools in those cities is a "handful." Not every district is underfunded. Not every teacher is overwhelmed. Not every school is falling apart. And no, reading and math scores don't need to jump in every classroom, attendance doesn't need to be worked on in every building—and students in our country's cities do *not* need to be saved.

But let's be staggeringly honest here: So many of the things we just described *are* the reality in so many of our city schools. So instead of pretending they aren't, let's talk about what *is* actually happening in those schools and what we can do about it.

Principals spend most of their days putting out fires and responding to little things that come up, like the parent who stops by the school unannounced and wants to discuss their son's grade in math. Because these "little things" pile up, principals find little time to spend in the classroom with teachers and students. They're often not driving their vision and values, not observing teachers, not setting and tracking goals, and just barely hanging on.

Sometimes, these leaders have great relationships with students. But what about other essential functions, such as engaging in meaningful instructional and culture walkthroughs; ensuring deans are completing behavior referrals; ensuring teachers are at their posts during arrival, dismissal, lunch, and transitions; running effective, agenda-driven leadership team meetings; engaging in daily leadership huddles; creating and facilitating high-impact, engaging training for the entire staff; and walking the building consistently to ferret out anything that doesn't meet their bar? These are not always happening. And as such, many leaders may not know what the bar actually *is*.

If they hear teachers speaking ill of families, they might not say anything. If they see three educational assistants on the playground huddled in a corner chatting, with their backs to students instead of monitoring them to ensure safety, they might not say anything. If they see students in the halls without passes, students out of uniform, and teachers who are wildly underprepared for class, they might not say anything. If they hear adults yelling at students, they might not make a peep.

Sometimes, the leaders do know these things are unacceptable. As a result, they might blame the adults for their lack of professionalism or blame the students for not meeting expectations. Instead of blaming others, as the leader, *they* need to own these issues.

Unshakable Leadership

The research is clear. School leaders are the most significant contributing factor to the success of a school. Research out of the Wallace Foundation (Grissom et al., 2021) found that "replacing a below-average principal (at the 25th percentile) with an above-average one (at the 75th percentile) would increase the typical student's learning by nearly three months in both math and reading annually" (p. 91). These findings underscore the importance of enhancing or supplementing leadership skills in urban schools as a crucial step in improving teaching and learning outcomes for students (Leithwood et al., 2004).

That is what this book is all about. We know that the impact of effective school leadership is far more pronounced in schools facing challenging conditions. In fact, school transformation *won't* occur in the absence of a strong leadership figure. Although various elements may play a role in these transformations, competent leadership is the essential driving force (Leithwood et al., 2004).

Unshakable leaders rarely miss things, and when they do, they own it. They don't take feedback personally; they use it to get better. They communicate early and often. They live by their calendars but are also responsive enough to act swiftly and precisely. They address anything that doesn't meet the bar, and they influence instruction through observation, feedback, and coaching.

These unshakable leaders get hit with challenges—sometimes challenges so big that they feel insurmountable. But despite this, they lean on their systems. They lean on their culture. They lean on their team. They may get hit, but they never crumble. Even when they want to.

Some professionals have the luxury of learning as they go, with limited negative repercussions. An accountant might make a mistake on someone's taxes, have to deal with the displeasure of a boss or client, and lose a weekend redoing the job. But once the changes are made, they're made, and the mistakes are forgotten.

Let's compare this with the principal who hasn't thought through the culture system in their school. Five teachers in one grade may have five different incentive systems. They may deliver consequences to students for misbehaviors in five different ways. The result? Students will be unsure of the expectations, and the principal will likely become frustrated with teacher inconsistency. In some cases, students will feel defeated, believing there's no point in trying to improve things. The negative repercussions of this lack of clarity will ripple through the school, affecting teacher trust in the administration, family trust in teachers, and student and teacher relationships.

The fact is, schools are more like hospitals or airlines than like accounting firms.

Hospitals and airlines are known as *high-reliability organizations*. They're places where, if people mess up, other people get hurt. There, precision counts, autonomy is low, alignment is sky-high, and accountability matters. Urban schools are the same: If people mess up, other people get hurt. They're also high-reliability organizations—or should be.

Why We Wrote This Book

Millions of us tune into both the summer and winter Olympics every two years, and despite the fact that almost none of us are or have been Olympic athletes, we're able to tell almost immediately when a figure-skating routine is medal worthy and when it's not. We know whether a sprinter got out of the blocks too slowly. We know when a dive is good because there's hardly a splash. And we groan when a gymnast ends their routine by taking the slightest step backward before raising their hands in triumph because we know there will be a deduction. In short, when it comes to the Olympics, we all know what "good" looks like.

Such clarity also exists about what "good" looks like in school: in instruction, culture, arrival and dismissal routines, lunch, assemblies, parent communications, and professional development. We can define what good looks like in schools as clearly as a coach can define a gymnast's routine. We can train our teams on these things, and when those things don't meet the bar, we can immediately notice—and we immediately make corrections.

We *should* and we *can*, but we rarely *do*.

We believe that any school leader, urban or otherwise, *can* get to this place where clarity, precision, alignment, and accountability exist. We're going to skip what curriculum you should use, and we're not going to write about social-emotional learning or restorative justice in this book. We'll leave conversations about DEI training and student trauma out as you can find myriad titles that go miles deep there. We'll also skip how you should navigate districtwide expectations that may misalign with what your schools actually need or how to manage relationships with sometimes prickly teachers' unions as well. These are *real* challenges, and they're not going anywhere. Still, leaders are thriving in the face of them.

Instead, we'll focus on crucial school processes, the role of the school leadership team, and high-quality instruction and coaching. We'll write about creating and sustaining a school culture system that staff members understand and that works for students. We'll walk you through 21 essential strategies that will help you transform your school.

We've bucketed these strategies into four categories: planning and preparation, teaching and coaching, school culture, and bringing it all to life. For each strategy, we'll begin with an anecdote of a time when its presence or absence played out. We'll describe why it matters and what best practices make it come to life. We'll list steps you can use to roll out the strategy to staff, and we'll include best practices for execution—how to sustain the strategy as long as necessary. Every chapter will conclude with possible pitfalls, as well as with an essential conversation model to use when someone on the team isn't operating in alignment with that strategy.

When applicable, we include special education considerations for you and your team to think about and act on throughout the book. Both of us have worked closely with special ed departments for years, and Michael taught special education at the beginning of his career. He is also the father of a profoundly autistic son and on the board of an autism nonprofit.

Special education teams, staff, and students are often the forgotten ones in schools. However, to have a truly effective, radically successful, transformational school, all staff and students, not just some or most, need to be included, elevated, and along for the ride, so we are including considerations for special education throughout the book. We are aware, though, that some of you reading this do not have special education departments. Please use what's helpful and disregard what's not.

We'll also assume that you have *some* help as a leader. You might have a large team or a small one, or it may be just you with an administrative assistant or a lead teacher. Please do not dismiss the coaching we're providing in this book because you think it might require 15 people to bring it to fruition. Whatever your circumstances, we invite you to make the coaching as relevant as you're able.

So let's begin. Even if you're only able to get to some of the 21 strategies, we promise you that change will occur.

PART I

Planning and Preparation

Create and Embody a School Vision

Recently, in our school vision trainings, we've begun adding a cartoon of a four-member rowing team. Two members of the team are rowing in one direction. Above their heads, a thought bubble appears with "social-emotional learning" inside it. The other two team members are rowing in the opposite direction. Above their heads, their thought bubble says, "student-centered learning." We then ask participants to reflect on whether their teams are "rowing in the same direction." School leaders report overwhelmingly, and a little embarrassed, that they aren't. But this is a good thing to find out because if they fail to address this, success will elude them forever.

This isn't to say that everyone needs to have the same focus daily. The director of operations, the director of special education, and the enrollment manager will have different objectives. However, it does mean that everyone understands what you are all trying to accomplish *on the macro level*—and that they make decisions based on that.

Take this recent example. At a school where some leaders claimed they were striving to have the best college preparatory school in their state, other leaders wouldn't get on board with asking teachers to submit their lesson plans for feedback—because they didn't want to upset the teachers. These two things cannot be true at the same time: We cannot say we want to have the best school in the state *and* that it's OK for teachers to go into their classrooms with less-than-stellar lesson plans that could have been greatly improved through feedback.

A lived school vision is like the North Star, guiding a school team, informing their actions, and getting them back on course when they've veered off of it. Every leader should know this vision by heart. Too often, though, leaders only have a sense of their school vision. But that's like your Uber driver only having a "sense" of where to drive you. It's something that's written in a handbook and maybe on a wall, but it's rarely, if ever, referenced.

Lived School Vision

What It Is

A lived school vision is an anchoring statement that speaks to what the school is intending to accomplish. It's aspirational, it's catchy, and it's something (this matters immensely) that's frequently referenced.

Why It Matters

Knowing where you're headed or attempting to head and then aligning everyone around that enables the team to row in the same direction, especially when rowing in opposite directions is so very easy to do.

Best Practices for Planning

Developing a shared, lived school vision is a leadership responsibility that requires care, collaboration, and continuous engagement with stakeholders. As Kotter (2012) emphasizes, "*Vision* refers to a picture of the future with some implicit or explicit commentary on why people should strive to create that future. . . . it helps coordinate the actions of different people, even thousands and thousands of individuals, in a remarkably fast and efficient way" (p. 71).

Your school or organization may already have a school vision that was created by a previous administration, your board, or you. If it's relevant and aspirational enough, if it appeals to your better self, that vision can remain in place. Now you may or may not be able to change your school's vision as a whole. It may be determined by a network or district, or it may require board approval to shift, but you *can* control the vision for the coming school year. Meaning, even if the larger vision feels irrelevant and out of touch, you can align the team around a shorter-term, more timely vision that might need to be revised next year or in a few years.

Keep the following in mind when clarifying your vision.

Be Future Oriented

Your vision should be an ideal state that is aspirational and forward thinking.

Paint a Picture

What does your ideal school look like and sound like? What is the vibe when people walk through the door? Painting a picture of your ideal school will help clarify your vision for staff members.

Don't Describe Numerical Success

You don't need to capture all the details of your ideal state. The vision, *We are the premier math and science middle school in the state of Illinois* is more compelling than, *Ninety percent of our students will score proficient or advanced on the Illinois State Assessment* (this is a goal, and we'll get there down the road).

Collaboratively Develop Your Vision

All good leaders should include the varied voices of their community. Regardless of whether you plan to overhaul your school vision entirely or create one for the year, taking the following steps will help ensure success.

1. **Establish a foundation for collaboration.** Assess the current state of your school and community, either alone or with a small group of leaders and teachers. Start with your purpose for existing. What problem are you trying to solve? What makes what

you're doing unique and special in the current education space? For instance, you may be leading a middle school that feeds into multiple high schools across the city, so you might include language about preparing students for their high school journey (and beyond). You might be leading a faith-based school and want to instill more faith-based identity into your scholars, so it would make sense to include this.

2. **Clearly define for everyone how this vision will shape school improvement and lead to student success.** Next, do a critical analysis of student data in the areas of achievement, school culture, and stakeholder engagement. Your vision process has to be informed by data even though your vision statement will not include those data.
3. **Engage in open discussion, and collaborate.** Peter Senge (2006) argues in one of his seminal textbooks on change management that "people don't resist change. They resist being changed" (p. 193). This reinforces the crucial importance of ensuring inclusivity. To facilitate inclusive meetings, have visioning sessions, as opposed to taking a workshop approach in which an entire group is tasked with engineering the language of a vision. That will likely end in chaos. By "visioning sessions," we're referring to focus groups, surveys, and facilitated collaborative meetings. During these meetings, engage stakeholders in a reflective dialogue where they address guiding questions, such as "What do we want our students to achieve?" "What do we need to do to be the best school in the city?" and "What's currently missing from our teaching and learning approach?"
4. **Create a clear and inspiring vision statement.** Once you've gathered all the feedback from stakeholders and worked with a small coalition to refine the vision, it's time to make the statement concise and memorable. As you wordsmith the vision statement, continually refer to the goals and broader educational priorities of your district and school community. For example,

   At Lucas High School, we provide a transformational educational experience to students of all abilities and backgrounds. We never waiver from empowering our students, families, and staff to achieve all that they are capable of, while providing A+ support and guidance every step of the way.

Best Practices for Staff Rollout

Now that you have your vision statement, it is time to communicate and roll out your vision to the community. Be sure to consider the following.

Expect Discomfort

Because the statement will not have captured everyone's thoughts and wishes, you will need to anticipate those trouble areas ahead of time. Preparing a strong rationale on the front end and relevant responses, also steeped in rationale, for when people push back will help build trust and consensus.

Exemplify the Vision

Do this through your actions, your school's accountability language, and celebrations. Embody the vision in your everyday interactions with the school community. This could look like, at our fictional Lucas High School, asking a student who may be struggling to complete their homework, "Kelly, what are the obstacles stopping you from completing it? As you know, part of our vision is around empowering students, so while I could *tell you* what I think, it'll be more aligned to what we're trying to accomplish for you to do some thinking on it first."

Distribute the Vision Statement and Create Visual Reminders

Share it in staff meetings, in newsletters, and on digital platforms. Display the vision prominently in classrooms and hallways, and reference it in all school communications.

Behavior is contagious. Reference the vision relentlessly to ensure the *right* behaviors are catching on.

Best Practices for Execution

Now that you've got the ball rolling, it's time to execute. Take note of the following.

Embed Your School Vision in Your Strategic Planning

The vision should connect everything from curriculum development and implementation to hiring and professional learning.

Align Your Vision

Be sure to align your vision with your teacher evaluation performance goals and metrics (we will talk about this in Chapter 18), as well as with your measurements of student progress and success.

Celebrate Wins and Progress

Recognize staff and student achievements aligned with the vision through awards, public acknowledgments, and student showcases. Oftentimes, even in very positive schools, when staff are recognized, it's without any connection to what the school says they care about (i.e., vision and values).

Regularly Reassess and Revise Your Vision

According to Fullan (2005), sustainable leadership is rooted in ensuring that a vision for change continues to evolve beyond the tenure of any single leader. If we believe that, then the work of promulgating a school vision cannot be static. The effective school leader must regularly reassess and refine their vision to maintain its relevance and impact. This process is strengthened through intentional structures such as vision committees, stakeholder focus groups, and surveys and questionnaires, which allow leaders to gather diverse perspectives and ensure the vision remains responsive to the changing needs of the school community.

Be mindful *not* to pivot simply because you haven't had success. This happens too often. If it's the "right" stuff, focus on different ways to execute, not changing because the current execution hasn't worked yet.

Think back to Lucas High School, whose current vision is *At Lucas High School, we provide a transformational educational experience to students of all abilities and backgrounds. We never waiver from empowering our students, families, and staff to achieve all that they are capable of, while providing A+ support and guidance every step of the way.*

The team at Lucas High might determine, after a few years of strong execution, that their students aren't as successful post–high school as they deserve to be. They might then begin to partner with local businesses who offer internships. They might work with local colleges to arrange tours and Q&A sessions. As a result, their vision might evolve to something like the below:

At Lucas High School, we provide a transformational educational experience to students of all abilities and backgrounds. We never waiver from empowering our students, families, and staff to achieve all that they are capable of, while providing A+ support and guidance every step of the way. ***We prepare our students for college and career through intentional teaching, coaching, and partnerships.***

Considerations for Special Education

Note: This information is relevant for Chapters 1 and 2.

All students learn differently. Some schools overlook this fact and will need to explicitly include students with disabilities in the school vision. They should define success in terms of access to grade-level instruction, meaningful participation, and progress toward ambitious goals, as research consistently links inclusive vision-setting to improved academic and social outcomes for students with disabilities (Ainscow et al., 2006; McLeskey et al., 2014).

Leaders must avoid overemphasizing special education as a separate department with separate systems. Use the school vision to drive overall structural decisions that include staffing, scheduling, service delivery models, and resource allocation when considering specialized service delivery. These actions ensure special education is aligned to core instructional priorities rather than operating as a parallel system (Billingsley et al., 2020).

Hold all educators accountable for students with disabilities, reinforcing shared ownership and high expectations, as collective responsibility and instructional coherence are strongly associated with improved outcomes in inclusive schools (Hattie, 2012; Klingner et al., 2015). Special education teachers are not the only folks responsible for the success of students with disabilities.

At every level, integrate special education into the core instructional system, including professional development, instructional coaching, and teacher evaluation, recognizing that sustained improvement depends on building general and special educators' shared capacity (Darling-Hammond et al., 2017).

The best leaders closely monitor alignment between the school vision and student experience by routinely reviewing inclusion rates, instructional quality, and progress toward individualized education plan (IEP) goals, using data to ensure that the lived experience of students with disabilities matches the school's stated commitments (McLaughlin & Rhim, 2007).

Common Pitfalls to Avoid

Of course, there are always pitfalls, so it is imperative to anticipate ones that might hinder the success of implementing a school vision.

A Disconnect Between Vision and Practice

A vision becomes ineffective when it lives in a theoretical space without actual integration into the daily practices, curriculum, and policies of the school and school culture. Marzano and colleagues (2005) encourage leaders to translate vision into action through aligning policies, managing resource allocation, and leading expert professional development. Look at all priorities, goals, teacher evaluations, student assessments, and professional learning initiatives through the lens of the school vision.

Fear of Change

Expect resistance when introducing or revising a school vision. Staff members may hesitate because of uncertainty, lack of trust, or previous experiences with unsuccessful initiatives. As Schein (2010) suggests, resistance is often rooted in perceived loss and emotional discomfort rather than opposition to improvement itself. To address this, proactively acknowledge concerns and create safe spaces for staff to share their questions and frustrations. Communicate openly about why changes are necessary and how the vision will be implemented. Be transparent about timelines, expectations, and decision-making processes. Most important, invite skeptical voices into the work by engaging them in planning, feedback sessions, and leadership roles. When staff members feel heard and included, resistance decreases and ownership increases.

About the Essential Conversation

To be clear, these conversations are about holding people accountable to what you care about as a school leader. According to a study from HR Dive (Starner, 2015), more than 80 percent of managers struggle with holding others accountable, and 91 percent of employees say it's one of their company's top leadership development needs. From our experience, this is because leaders haven't clearly defined what matters in their schools, so either they avoid asking people to meet expectations that don't exist or, when they do, it goes poorly.

To begin with, never ambush a staff member when you're looking to offer feedback; always preface the conversation with some kind of pressure test to ensure that the person is open to receiving it at that specific time. Of course, the time will nearly *always* be right from your perspective.

School can be stressful. Life can be stressful. Conditions will never be perfect. If the person got a flat tire on the way to work, have the conversation. If their cat is sick, have the conversation. If they just received a call that someone dear to them has passed away, you might want to wait. Always begin by asking, "Can I give you some feedback?" The person will most likely let you know if they're feeling receptive or not.

Second, anchor these conversations in a previously agreed-on expectation. For this example, referencing the school vision is perfect. "Mr. Phillips, as a reminder, at Lucas High School, part of our vision states that we provide a transformational educational experience to students of *all* abilities and backgrounds. So when you. . . ."

This is a game changer. Otherwise, you're like the person waiting at the airport, bags in hand, leaving frustrated messages on the cell phone of the friend you thought was going to pick you up but who, because of a communication glitch, never had any idea you were even coming to town.

Finally, conclude your conversation by cementing expectations and requesting that the other person reach out if they need support.

An Essential Conversation About Creating and Embodying School Vision

Questions to Keep in Mind

- What does "good" look like?
- Are people clear about that?
- Are people meeting that bar?
- Where are the gaps?
- What do I need to address immediately?

The Context: A teacher blames a student's family for "not caring."

The Essential Conversation

"Good morning, Mr. Smith. Can I share some feedback with you? Great! In yesterday's grade team meeting, you made reference to a student's family not caring about their child's education because it's been difficult for you to connect with them. But as you shared out, you called one phone number two times. As referenced in our vision statement, we provide *A+* support and guidance every step of the way for our students, fellow staff, and families. Your comment and actions did not embody this part of our vision. If you need support going forward, please reach out to me, but please refrain from using language that is antithetical to what we believe as a school, and please continue trying, even when the first couple of attempts haven't worked out. Does that resonate with you? Thanks!"

Our Rationale

This conversation with Mr. Smith may seem harsh and even unnecessary to some of you. You might think, "This person works really hard, and they only had a slip-up. What's the big deal? And if it *is* a big deal, shouldn't we be leading from a place of understanding? Shouldn't the conversation sound more like, 'Hey, is something wrong? I noticed you weren't yourself yesterday.'"

At Skyrocket, we preach the idea of *logical flexibility*. If this person truly performs at an *A+* level at all times and just had a simple miss, sure, have the second kind of conversation with them. However, from our experience, that's rarely the case. Usually fair to good employees operate in ways that are misaligned with expectations. When leaders don't address that misalignment, it makes matters worse because they're essentially cosigning that behavior. Either that or they spend an inordinate amount of time beating around the bush with the person who's out of alignment.

Now, of course you should care about every person on your team. If they're struggling, you should know about it and support them. But when it comes to being out of alignment with the school's expectations, it's rarely this complicated. A person is gossiping, not because their dog is sick or because of another complication in their life, but because expectations around addressing an issue by going straight to the source are lacking or because those expectations are not being reinforced and followed up on. Use logical flexibility when needed, but address everything else this succinctly.

2

Define and Live School Values

We read something recently where a leader shared the idea that creating a strong culture isn't about designing fancy vision statements or perfectly curated values. Instead, it's about making sure everyone on the staff and the entire student body feels seen, heard, and loved.

This is a nice sentiment, and we have no doubt that it comes from a good place. The problem is, it doesn't actually mean anything. At least, it doesn't mean the same thing to everyone on that leadership team, teaching staff, or student body.

Quick: Think about what it would look like to ensure your teaching staff feels "loved." What about making sure your student body feels "seen"? Certainly, you can come up with some ideas. But when we speak in generalities, when we say things like "nothing matters more than making people feel heard," we need to define what that looks like. Then we need to reinforce it relentlessly. We need to embody it fully. Otherwise, it becomes a thing that school leaders say they care about, but that staff members never actually feel or even are aware of in the daily life of the school.

A few months back, a leader asked us to help hold her team more accountable. We were happy to oblige, but before we started, we asked her if the school had any core values or tenets that they'd shared with staff. "Let me go onto the website," she replied, "so I can find them." You wouldn't want your child's doctor to have to go to a website to remember what the symptoms of strep throat are. Similarly, we haven't seen an example of a leader who *doesn't even know* their school's values being capable of leading their team or school in an aligned and a meaningful way.

When leaders are impeccably clear about what matters, they share that information with staff, garner buy-in, ask for feedback, get to a place of alignment around what those values look like in practice, and then repeatedly reference them. By doing so, they're creating and reinforcing an agreement. When this happens, their actions and their teachers' actions change.

Unfortunately, most school leaders *don't* do these things, resulting in a lack of productivity, confusion, infighting, frustration, and sometimes toxic work environments where unpredictability rules. Sure, they might have the larger vision statement we wrote about in Chapter 1, but those are bigger picture and more aspirational. Values get into the details of the day-to-day way staff should operate in service of the vision. These are *not* as granular as the adult expectations that come next, which are about things like how you dress, what time you arrive, or when lesson plans are due, but they are the behaviors you uphold, the ways in which you interact with each other, and how you carry yourself. Things like, we always look for solutions, we listen first, and we go straight to the source when there's an issue.

Some leaders will say that telling professionals what to do is unnecessary, patronizing, or even demeaning. We disagree. We believe it's the most fair and supportive thing a leader can do. It's something every individual deserves and every team craves.

This is where designing lived values comes in.

Lived Values

What They Are
Lived values are a set of memorable, aspirational words followed by brief descriptors (two to four sentences) that outline what those words mean in your context.

Why They Matter
To be a truly great team, alignment is paramount. Everyone must be clear on what matters—and clear on how to operate in service of what matters.

Best Practices for Planning

Best practices for planning begin with listing, drafting, and defining.

List What Matters

Are you focused on ensuring your students become effective problem solvers? On prioritizing student success over everything else? These can't be buzzwords or recycled jargon. They need to reflect what the school leader genuinely believes is essential for their school.

Sometimes, they can be born out of the vision statement. For example, Lucas High strives to provide a "transformational educational experience" to all students, so it could make sense to list "transformation" or even "transformational education" as a value. What comes next, however, is where this all comes to life.

Draft Values

Turn these ideas into catchy values that staff and students (if you choose for your values to be student-facing as well) that people will remember. Prioritizing problem solving might become "We Find a Way," and prioritizing student success, "Kids First."

Define What Matters

This distinction is wildly important. Often, teams will *list* what matters, but they won't go to the next step of defining what those things actually mean. For instance, a school will say "innovation" matters, but staff members, when asked, can't say what that looks like. Turn these big ideas into tangible, digestible pieces. For instance, if you list integrity as something that matters, what actions would you take as people of integrity? Perhaps, "We do what we say we do. We keep our word. We're there for others. We meet deadlines." A staff meeting is the perfect place for all staff to define what matters.

Best Practices for Staff Rollout

Now it's time to present these values to the teaching and culture staff, share the rationale for their selection, and invite feedback, which may range from making minor language tweaks to addressing wholesale oversights. Then engage the staff in a robust "Looks Like/Sounds Like" exercise where they reflect on the values and make a list of what they believe these values will look and sound like in practice. They might say, for example, that Every Student Every Day means you call on every child, not just those with raised hands or who are confident with the content. It might mean you know what each student's strengths and weaknesses are and you attend to those. It might mean that you conference with any student whose grades are below X to offer support.

Once this is done, you'll need to codify these ideas, remove redundancies, tighten language, and present them back to staff. Remember, *they*—not you—created the descriptors. So when there's a failing student in their class and the teacher is resisting providing additional support, you get to say, "Remember our value of Every Student Every Day. That means we know what all our kiddos need and we do everything we can to provide it."

Best Practices for Execution

Creating values is great, but it's more a beginning than an ending. Now that agreement about what matters is strong, it's time for expectations to come to life. The team will shift from a static set of words and phrases to something that everyone has internalized, pondered, and put mental energy into improving. Values should be referenced at the beginning of every one-on-one meeting, every leadership team meeting, and every staff meeting. Leaders should ask, "Where are *you* embodying these values? Be specific. Where can you do better? Be specific."

Ask for share-outs. Call on people who haven't yet contributed their thoughts so that you hear a variety of voices. Ask probing questions like "So which value does that align with?" Ask staff members to give a shout-out when their peers have reflected these values, both at meetings and through email.

Have a Values Wall in the school that lists your values. Each month, post photos of different students and staff members who have acted in service of those values. Include a values section on your evaluations, and use specific language from the values descriptions when providing both positive and constructive feedback.

We've seen so many examples of struggling to average staff who are all in on what the school cares about. These folks should be noticed and praised (and coached to be better, which is coming), as they are major assets to the team. All of this allows you to do that versus *only* focusing on performance.

Common Pitfalls to Avoid

Be alert to the following two pitfalls.

A Failure to Message Values

It's a major mistake to spend a lot of time creating and messaging values in the summer, only to stop referencing them after that. Unfortunately, many teams fall victim to this. They send email updates without any connection to values; they give shout-outs but never say a word about how the action described reflected the values; they begin meetings, hold assemblies, and run professional development sessions, all without saying anything about values. Values only live when they are messaged relentlessly. Otherwise, they go away.

Believing You Always Have to Agree

Having lived values doesn't mean you always agree on everything. Two assistant principals at the same school might disagree about the best approach to ensuring students buy in to a new initiative. But what they won't disagree about is whether having student buy-in matters in the first place because they've already decided that "we value student input." A teacher and a dean might debate the most effective way to communicate something to families, but they won't debate whether it's important to communicate with families because it's already been decided that "parents are our partners." And a dozen teachers might loathe a new system that's been proposed, but instead of gossiping about it and being resistant, they'll speak directly to leadership about it because at their school, "we go to the source." And they'll suggest some better options because it's expected that "we solve problems when they arise."

Our Skyrocket Values

Over the years at Skyrocket, we've received quite a bit of positive feedback about our own values, which we've listed below. If they're helpful, please adopt any one (or more) of them:

- **Mission first.** We operate without ego or personal pride. All decisions we make are in the best interest of Skyrocket, our partners, and our mission.
- **Radical transparency.** Anyone can give feedback to anyone on anything. We go straight to the source and deliver feedback with the intention of improving performance and outcomes.
- **Sky-high integrity.** We show up early, meet deadlines, and overdeliver on projects and deliverables; when we fall short, we own it and recommit.
- **Find a way.** When a problem arises, we commit to being bigger than our feelings and work to find solutions immediately.
- **Keep it simple.** We believe that less is more. We don't overcomplicate things. From conversations, to presentations, to every interaction, we prioritize simplicity.

- **Unwavering belief.** We believe unwaveringly in the ability and potential of our partners, their students, and their communities. We hold ourselves and our partners highly accountable for using language and exhibiting mindsets that reflect this.

An Essential Conversation About Defining Lived Values

Questions to Keep in Mind

- What does "good" look like?
- Are people clear about that?
- Are people meeting that bar?
- Where are the gaps?
- What do I need to address immediately?

The Context: The principal has overheard a teacher yelling at a student.

The Essential Conversation

"Good morning, Ms. Kelly. Do you have a moment? Great. Earlier today, I noticed you raising your voice to a student in the hallway. Although I imagine he frustrated you, our very first value is 'student safety is paramount.' When we raise our voices to kids, we're not contributing to a safe environment for them. You can rely on various systems and seek out coaching when you need support, but I want to ensure we're aligned going forward. Please do not raise your voice to students in the future. Does that make sense? Thank you for your time."

3

Clarify and Communicate Adult Expectations

To distinguish *adult expectations*—the topic of this chapter—from *lived values*, let's imagine the following scenario. Unshakable Air, a fictional airline company, touts the following values: customers first, safety above all, details matter, and representing the brand. As discussed, they'll need to define what those values look like in practice. For example, "customers first" might mean doing whatever it takes to ensure customers are happy. Things like greeting everyone with a smile, listening to concerns to understand and not to argue, and never letting anyone see you stressed out—even if the plane is delayed three hours or if it's bouncing side to side through a storm. "Safety above all" might mean that they always put their passenger safety first, even if it makes them unhappy when there's a storm cancellation or minor technical issue. Lived values define how they'll act in service of their vision.

Adult expectations are the various transactional responsibilities you simply need to do to be successful. At the airline, they'd be things like filling ice buckets 30 minutes before takeoff, queuing up safety videos right after the boarding door closes, or serving drinks to first-class passengers before takeoff. At a school, they might be things like lesson plans being due at noon on Fridays, teachers needing to call a minimum of seven families per week, deans responding to referrals within 24 hours, and everyone being on time (or communicating if they're going to be late).

Lived values govern how you operate. Adult expectations are *the tasks* you complete along the way in service of those values. Sometimes it'll feel like there's overlap. At Skyrocket, for instance, one of our values is sky-high integrity. It essentially means that we do what we say we'll do. That might mean meeting deadlines, showing up on time, and so on. But it's more general than the actions someone on the team will take every single day. For instance, our team also needs to have their calendars updated for the following week by Friday at 4 p.m. ET of the previous week. They also must have sign-ins from partner schools submitted by the first of every month for the previous month. These tasks are the adult expectations. They're upholding our values when they meet them.

Adult Expectations

What They Are

These refer to clear and precise expectations for all of the transactional things that adults in your building are expected to do every day. Some additional examples include updating gradebooks weekly, having emergency lesson plans on hand if one calls out sick, adults being in doorways during transitions, and so on.

Why They Matter

Leaders often think their teams will simply do the things the leader wants them to do without spelling out to them their need to actually do them. This is inefficient and leads to frustration for everyone. Don't assume that staff members know they should respond to emails within 24 hours. Explicitly *tell* them they should. Without expectations, accountability is nearly impossible. We waste so much time hoping that people will do what we want them to do when we never made it clear to begin with, and then we wonder why they didn't ever do them.

Best Practices for Planning

Expert planning for and setting of adult expectations require a thoughtful, transparent, and collaborative approach. Here's a structured way to do this.

Clarify Expectations

All adult expectations must be aligned with and reflect the school's vision, lived values, and goals (more on this later). There should be a clear connection between what is expected of the adults in your building and how that will drive you all toward success. Expectations should be ultra-clear and free of jargon-filled language, and they should precisely define what is expected of adults in terms of professionalism, communication, collaboration, instructional support, and student interactions. The bar for expectations should be high yet achievable. This allows for accountability to foster growth. Expectations need to be both rigorous and realistic; if they're not, buy-in will falter.

Communicate Expectations

We can't overemphasize the criticality of communicating and over-communicating expectations to your team. When it comes to expectations, we tell leaders to communicate them, then communicate them again—and then again and again and again. An old advertising adage says that people need to hear things seven times before they start to really internalize them. Communicating expectations must occur relentlessly through multiple channels and must be reinforced regularly.

An often-forgotten mode of communication is *modeling*. As the leader, you should exemplify the expectations you expect others to uphold every day.

Recently, a partner school was having issues with staff arriving on time. The principal decided to post a sign-in sheet next to his office, and he asked that staff sign in when they arrived. It was an imperfect system, because a person could fudge the time but only so much as it couldn't be earlier than the person who signed in before them. Still, it was a system and an attempt to reinforce an expectation. A frustrated teacher asked why the principal and the AP weren't signing in as well. The principal got offended and refused.

Initiative over.

Hold People Accountable

You've created clear expectations. You also have a system of consistent communication in place. Now you have to hold folks accountable.

- **Set aligned and measurable goals.** Tie expectations to observable and measurable outcomes. Be sure to share those goals and all progress monitoring of those goals with the appropriate stakeholders. For example, in a weekly newsletter, list the average daily attendance of staff for that week or the percentage of teachers who turned in exemplar lesson plans.
- **Address noncompliance promptly.** When expectations are not being met, you should have a clear process for how to address any lapse from the team (we'll address this in Chapter 12). This might involve coaching, other supports, or even corrective action. But if a teacher's assistant on lunch duty is on their phone and that's misaligned with the schoolwide expectations, you need to address it immediately. Otherwise, that behavior could become contagious. (As a note, we're not writing about the person with a sick child at home who's sending a quick text and then is right back to engaging with and actively monitoring students. We're talking about the person on Instagram who has no idea you're even in the lunchroom observing. Use logical flexibility.)
- **Use data and feedback.** Collect data regularly from your staff about their understanding of and their belief in the expectations. Use evaluations, surveys, and performance reviews to collect data and to give and get formative feedback about how folks are being held accountable to expectations.

Best Practices for Staff Rollout

Keep the following in mind as you take this next step.

Share Clear and Aligned Expectations

Begin by anchoring adult expectations in what you say you care about. As referenced earlier, there should be a clear line between what you outline as expectations for adults in the building and the organization's vision, values, and goals. When outlining expectations, ensure they are precise and observable. Some may be role specific. That's OK. Use clear, action-oriented language. For example, use "Arrive on time, prepared for all meetings" instead of "Be punctual and professional." You could define "prepared" more clearly for newer staff: "This means laptops charged, pen and paper available, phone on silent."

If this level of detail feels like you'd be micromanaging, we'll share the story of a rock star coach on our team who showed up late and with a dead computer to their very first meeting with Michael and a new leader they'd be coaching. That coach then held up the meeting even further and knocked into things to stretch their computer cord all over the room. An experienced, amazing, brilliant leader did this, so is it crazy that a brand-new dean might need to be told to tuck in their shirt?

One note here is that you should choose wisely what you're going to ask your team to do. You've likely heard the expression "If everything matters, nothing does." What would be nice, but it's not the most important thing? Too many schools who engage in this try to do *everything*. They have dozens of expectations that simply become noise and ultimately fade away because no one can possibly keep track of them all. Choose wisely.

Launch with Intention

Use designated meeting time, retreats, or a well-thought-out memo (just as a precursor—you'll want to share these in person so they stick) to introduce expectations as part of a larger vision for culture and effectiveness. Reinforce the message on posters and in emails, handbooks, and one-on-one conversations. Leaders must continually repeat and revisit the expectations. Regularly circle back to expectations in team huddles or professional development sessions because repetition helps build internalization.

Provide Support and Accountability

During the rollout phase, be sure to offer substantive resources, including training, coaching, and feedback loops, to help adults meet and maintain expectations. Leaders should always approach misalignment with a growth mindset, assuming the best and leading with support as their starting point. When needed, enforce expectations consistently with fair feedback and consequences.

Best Practices for Execution

You've made it to the execution phase. Now consider the following.

Collaborate

Once launched, create a space for open dialogue. What's working? What's not? To be clear, not What's hard? or What's annoying? Take the time to hold genuine conversations. Are you asking teachers to walk students from the first floor to the fourth floor while also using every minute of their instruction and not being late to next period? Staff members must be comfortable asking for clarification and providing feedback to you and your team on how well they—and you—are meeting those expectations. Avoid top-down dictates.

Celebrate the Wins

The old mindset about not praising folks for "doing their job" or for doing what they "should be doing" is outdated and frankly poor leadership. Acknowledge excellence in shout-outs, awards, and personalized notes to highlight the importance of meeting expectations, and reinforce that this is really important to you as the leader, the school, and the students.

Offer High Support

Provide ongoing support and resources to ensure that adults are meeting expectations and fulfilling the school's vision. Ensure there is ongoing professional development when trend data dictate a need to address an ongoing gap in expectations. For instance, you say that Wednesday PD starts at 2:30 p.m. sharp, but each of the past three weeks you have seen an increase in both staff arriving late and some not showing up at all. Make it easy for folks to meet expectations by providing the appropriate time, technology, and tools to be successful. If the tools have been provided, reset expectations and have essential conversations to reinforce them.

Considerations for Special Education

Note: This information is relevant for Chapters 3 and 4.

Without hesitation, articulate the nonnegotiable expectations for serving students with disabilities, including instructional rigor, implementation of IEP accommodations, and use of evidence-based practices. Clarity around these expectations is strongly linked to improved fidelity and student outcomes (Cook & Odom, 2013; McLeskey et al., 2014).

Communicate that the responsibility for students with disabilities is shared, not siloed. Do not shy away from explicitly proclaiming the roles of general educators, special educators, leaders, and support staff in support of students with disabilities. This stance reinforces collective accountability as a driver of inclusive school effectiveness (Billingsley et al., 2020; Klingner et al., 2015).

Anchor feedback and coaching conversations (discussed in Chapter 7) in clearly defined expectations, using the school vision and adult expectations to address inconsistent practices, particularly when instruction or compliance falls short for students with IEPs (Fixsen et al., 2005).

Monitor and reinforce expectations through consistent follow-up, using walkthroughs, data reviews, and supervision to ensure adult actions align with communicated expectations and legal obligations to students with disabilities (McLaughlin & Rhim, 2007).

Common Pitfalls to Avoid

Leaders should avoid the following pitfalls as they ensure accountability to a high bar.

Lack of Clarity

Lack of clarity might refer to conflicting messages from leadership or inconsistency in how the expectation is addressed and enforced. Clearly define, communicate, and reinforce your expectations for the staff.

Fears About Workload and Burnout

Staff members are busy. You may feel that requiring adults to meet various expectations is adding on to their already loaded job responsibilities. You might think that "taking it easy" on them is the right thing to do. Although leaders must be attuned to the potential for emotional exhaustion because of high student needs, challenging behaviors, or administrative demands, never lower the bar. Doing so actually leads to more struggle, frustration, and resentment as things start slipping and unpredictability reigns.

Lack of Leadership Modeling and Inconsistent Accountability

This can occur when leaders are not modeling the expectations they set for their staff. They may hold some individuals accountable but not others. School leaders must be the living embodiment of their expectations and of their overall vision for their school. Always enforce expectations equally (see Figure 3.1).

Figure 3.1

Expectations: What Do They Actually Look Like?

Here's a list of various adult expectations that leaders should consider clarifying for their staff:

- **Punctuality and attendance.** What does "on time" mean? What duties and meetings require attendance?
- **Dress code compliance.** What does a "professional and appropriate appearance" mean?
- **Preparedness.** What should staff be doing to prepare for daily responsibilities, such as lesson plans and meetings?
- **Confidentiality.** How will staff members protect student and staff privacy in compliance with laws and policies?
- **Team participation.** What are the expectations around engaging in team meetings, committees, and school initiatives?
- **Timely responses.** What are the expectations in terms of timeliness around addressing emails, phone calls, and messages?
- **Health and safety compliance.** What are the school safety protocols and procedures?
- **Technology use.** What is appropriate school technology use?
- **Time off.** What is the process for calling out? Do teachers need to have emergency lesson plans for subs? Can they take off before or after holidays?

An Essential Conversation About Clarifying and Communicating Adult Expectations

Questions to Keep in Mind

- What does "good" look like?
- Are people clear about that?
- Are people meeting that bar?
- Where are the gaps?
- What do I need to address immediately?

The Context: The principal addresses the need for full engagement in professional development.

The Essential Conversation

"Good afternoon, Dr. Linder. I have some feedback I'd like to share with you. Are you open to that? Great. In yesterday's professional development, you refused to engage with your group. When Assistant Principal Smith approached you about it, she said you responded with 'I do my work by myself. I don't need to do it now.' Is that accurate?"

"Mostly. I never miss a deadline, and I haven't in 18 years. I like working at home, where it's silent, and where I can be focused on my work. Being forced to do it in a room of 50 adults feels patronizing and unnecessary. I'd rather grade papers during that time instead of working with anyone else."

"Got it. I appreciate your transparency. Dr. Linder, as a reminder, one of our nonnegotiable adult expectations is full participation in professional development. When you refuse to engage, you're not meeting that expectation. Now, you've been here for nearly two decades, so I get that it may feel like you've done this before, but there's a bigger picture I want us to consider. There are 15 teachers on our team who have fewer than three years of experience each. And in your content area, which is the group with whom you were working yesterday, there are five teachers who are in their first year. These folks are looking to veterans like yourself for guidance and inspiration. If you

(continued)

express disinterest in this kind of collaboration and participation, they may, too. That will ultimately hurt our culture. Between our expectation of full participation and our value of being a model of excellence, your actions yesterday didn't meet either.

"Going forward, I'm going to continue to expect that you'll work with your group and that you'll model full participation for them. Can I count on you to engage going forward?"

Our Rationale

This example may seem extreme to some of you. Because is it really a big deal if Dr. Linder likes to do his work at home instead of in a cafeteria with a bunch of people who were in elementary school when he started teaching? Maybe not. But what if that person also doesn't like submitting lesson plans? Or having you, as the principal, in their classroom? What if they think that posting the day's objective is a stupid waste of time? How far are you, as a leader, willing to bend? Will you *only* bend on their "working at home" request—but hold the bar sky-high for everything else? What if three other people begin doing the same? What if a group of 10 decide to no longer even show up for PD?

Moreover, are you saying that it's important for other teachers to meet this expectation but not Dr. Linder? You must hold Dr. Linder to this expectation or you risk a complete culture breakdown, which, if you're reading this book, you certainly do not want.

4

Define and Disseminate Roles and Responsibilities

Years ago, we were coaching a leadership team in Delaware. On arriving at the school one day, the assistant principal pulled us into his office, saying, "I need your help in speaking to the principal." When we asked what happened, he replied, "She totally undermined me!"

As it turns out, the school had a field trip scheduled about 45 minutes from the building. That location just so happened to be a few minutes from the house of one of the teachers, who asked the assistant principal (AP) if it was OK if she just drove her car to the field trip and then directly home afterward. Going on the bus would take her an additional two hours to get home.

Although the AP appreciated the teacher's request, he stated that part of her job was to support students on the bus. If she drove, she'd be unable to do that. He also believed that approving the request could set a precedent that for every field trip, he would hear from multiple teachers who'd rather drive or take the train or maybe not go at all. So he said no and explained why.

The teacher didn't like this response, so she asked the principal, without mentioning that she'd already spoken to the AP. The principal didn't see an issue and said yes.

The AP wanted coaching on how to address this with both the principal and the teacher. We said we could support him in this, but we first asked, "Whose job is it to handle field trip logistics?"

"Well, we both kind of do it," he replied. In actuality, that means that *no one* truly does this job and that every decision is a crapshoot.

Roles and Responsibilities

What They Are

These encompass the clearly defined roles and corresponding tasks for all school leadership. Every single area should have one person who runs lead (even if there are multiple people who support that person). These roles should be memorialized in a document or one-pager.

Why They Matter

Sometimes creating roles and responsibilities may feel like you are inferring that you don't usually get the help you need from your colleagues and, therefore, that you need to formally stipulate it. That is not the case at all. In fact, it's the exact opposite. When roles are clear and people know what they're accountable for, it's easier for them to offer support to people on their team because they're not just running around doing whatever comes up in the moment. You need to make sure folks know what their roles entail—what's in their bucket and what is not. There's been so much strife in the history of schools because one person had no idea why another person did something that was not their responsibility, was not in their bucket, and which they really had no business even getting involved in.

Best Practices for Planning

Assigning roles and responsibilities within a school requires strategic thinking and clear communication. Maximizing team effectiveness is the name of the game here. To begin with, each role should have a clearly defined scope that includes key responsibilities and any decision-making authority. This scope is typically detailed in the job description, but it usually requires some refinement. The description should also outline measurable goals: what success looks like and how it will be measured.

Align Responsibilities with Priorities and Expertise

Start with the school's priorities; name them, and clarify who will lead the initiative. For example, the priority for the year may be increasing adult and student joy. Instead of saying, "That's everyone's responsibility," assign a specific leader to lead that priority. Clarify that although that leader will not be responsible for all aspects of the priority, they *will* be responsible for its overall implementation and eventual success. Consider, also, how responsibilities match with and leverage individuals' strengths, expertise, and passions.

Let's look at this in more detail:

- **Prioritize.** Focus on areas that get you close to your vision and help you meet your goals, such as improving student achievement, fostering teacher growth, and engaging families and the community.
- **Balance the workload.** Distribute the workload equitably. Don't put the burden of success on a few individuals, leaving others with lighter, less consequential workloads.
- **Ensure teamwork.** Assign responsibilities in a way that fosters teamwork by ensuring that the responsibilities span different departments.
- **Focus on strengths.** Use a strengths-based assessment tool, such as Gallup's CliftonStrengths (www.gallup.com/cliftonstrengths/en/home.aspx) or DISC (https://onlinediscprofile.com) to provide a data-driven aspect to delegating responsibilities.

Communicate Clearly and Transparently

Nothing is more important than clear communication when it comes to defining the roles and responsibilities within a school community, especially at the leadership level.

- **Create a leadership playbook.** Start by publishing a modified organizational chart, which we'll refer to as a *leadership playbook* (see Figure 4.1 for an example). This should be a visual representation that clarifies reporting structures, as well as the responsibilities of each leader. Distribute the playbook to all members of the community.
- **Reinforce responsibilities.** During leadership meetings, review who is responsible for what. Reinforce collective goals, and clarify and reiterate expectations for the team.
- **Align and track goals.** Confirm that all roles and responsibilities include aligned and measurable goals that monitor success and predict challenges. Using the SMART approach to goal setting—goals need to be specific, measurable, achievable, relevant, and time bound—is an easy way to track performance. Ensure that regular check-ins are providing staff members with ongoing feedback and support.

Best Practices for Staff Rollout

The rollout for roles and responsibilities needs to happen in four stages.

Stage 1. Clarify Who's Doing What

Present team members with drafts of what you believe they're responsible for. Ask them for feedback on what feels aligned to what they're currently doing and what seems new and might need an explanation. Also, get feedback on things they're currently doing that are *not* reflected in the document. School leaders often just pick up a random task, either because there was a gap when someone else left or because it just fell into their lap. You need to know what everyone is actually doing. Some of those tasks may stay. Some will already have been bucketed to someone else. And some will need to be bucketed to someone else after the meeting is over.

Stage 2. Check in First, Then Formally Present

Imagine, for instance, that your assistant principal is tired of handling the testing calendar. If you simply present that task as part of the AP's roles and responsibilities, they may push back in the meeting and declare, "I'm not doing that anymore!" You now have a choice: You can either power through and risk upsetting that person or abruptly shift the task to someone else, a someone else who might not want to take it on.

Ultimately, you're the decision maker. You can't possibly operate your school based on what people like. However, someone may have a genuine concern about a role you might assign them (Michael has joked that he could build a rocket to Jupiter before he could create a MAP testing schedule). So although you will have already gotten clarity around who is doing what (Stage 1), once your decisions are "final," it's best to check in with everyone to ensure alignment.

Gather information and make any needed changes in private. This way, the final group meeting in which you formally present the document will be more of a "for your information" meeting than breaking news.

Stage 3. Present the Final Doc to Leaders

There aren't a lot of easy leadership moves, but this is one. By this point, you will have gotten clarity about who's doing what, created roles and responsibilities for the upcoming year, received feedback individually from all leaders, and made any changes necessary. This meeting is simply presenting this document, not for feedback because that has already happened, but as a finalized resource.

In this meeting, however, it will make sense to ask leaders to partner up with people they'll both need support from and provide support to. They can begin to set meetings and plan out their work together. Some things will take precedence: Designing your bus drop-off and pick-up system will matter more than the logistics for the end-of-year dance that's happening in nine months.

Stage 4. Share Relevant Information with the Entire Staff

It's preferable to present staff with a revised document that only shows information they actually need to know. They probably don't need to know who's responsible for creating the formal evaluation calendar or who schedules interviews for potential new employees. However, they *do* need to know who to submit their lesson plans to, who their dean is, who handles field trips and assemblies, and so on. Ensure that all staff members have physical copies of the document; give them time to process the information and ask questions. It's essential to reinforce the need for them to go to the right people for the right reason.

You might mention that if staff members *do* go to the incorrect person, they'll be redirected to the person they were supposed to see. This may feel cold and unfeeling at times. Imagine, for instance, telling a struggling teacher who hesitantly approaches their AP to ask for assistance that they actually need to see their dean.

We get it. That's tough. Use logical flexibility. But think about everything you'll gain: People will be more inclined to stay in their lanes, there will be less sharing of nonurgent needs with whichever leader is closest at hand, and there will be far less frustration.

Best Practices for Execution

Figure 4.1 shows an example of a staff-facing leadership playbook. It lists the possible members of a leadership team, and lets staff know which responsibilities rest with which leader.

Common Pitfalls to Avoid

Avoid the following associated with roles and expectations.

Unclear Job Descriptions and Mismatched Roles

Unclear job descriptions can lead to confusion about daily activities and responsibilities. If Ms. Liston is "in charge" of culture, she might not

Figure 4.1

Example of a Leadership Playbook

Role	Key Responsibilities
Principal	Oversees overall school leadership, vision setting, stakeholder engagement, and accountability
Assistant Principal (Instruction)	Oversees curriculum, instruction, and teacher professional development
Assistant Principal (Student Services)	Manages student behavior, support services, and social-emotional learning initiatives
Director of Operations	Handles facilities, transportation, safety, and logistical support
Director of Special Education	Ensures compliance, accommodations, and supports for students with disabilities
Dean of Students	Focuses on student celebrations, discipline, culture, and attendance
Director of Family and Community Engagement	Strengthens partnerships with families and community stakeholders
Instructional Coach	Directly coaches teachers, provides curricula resources and support, and designs and delivers professional development

totally know what that means, whereas if Ms. Liston handles all assemblies, attendance and tardy tracking, student shout-outs, and processing referrals, she is clear about her responsibilities.

Staff members may end up in roles that are not well suited for them. As we wrote about earlier, some leaders will name this upfront, but others may not know or may be hesitant to share. This can lead to an increased reliance on management and to feelings of being ineffective. Switching roles midyear may make sense, but be mindful of the other person and what they'll now be taking on and giving up. What mostly happens is that the principal just takes on that person's responsibilities. They think, "I'm already *mostly* doing this job for them anyway. And to be honest, I'm better at it than them. It's just easier if I do it." But then they do it for others—leading to the job being untenable. It's better to coach that struggling person up instead.

An Essential Conversation About Defining and Disseminating Roles and Expectations

Questions to Keep in Mind

- What does "good" look like?
- Are people clear about that?
- Are people meeting that bar?
- Where are the gaps?
- What do I need to address immediately?

The Context: The principal clarifies the importance of knowing who to go to in school and for what.

The Essential Conversation

"Good morning, Theresa. Can I share some feedback with you? I was made aware that you approached Ms. Cummings about requesting time off next month. Ms. Cummings took your request to the person who's responsible for processing time-off requests, Ms. Thiessen. Because Ms. Thiessen was unclear on exactly what you were asking, she had to reach back out to you about it. As you know, one of our values is 'keeping it simple.' When you went to Ms. Cummings, it led to miscommunication and extra communication to clear it up, with all three of you doing additional and unnecessary work.

"Going forward, please ensure you're going to the correct person for any asks or needs. If you're unsure whom to go to, please refer to the roles and responsibilities chart. Can I count on you to do that? Thanks so much."

5

Exemplify Effective Communication

We were at a school in Chicago a couple of years back meeting with a principal, when a very pregnant teacher knocked on the door. The principal, who suddenly realized she had scheduled a meeting with that teacher at that time, waved the woman in and blurted out, "Oh, I can't meet now. I'll follow up with some suggested new times."

The principal wanted to return to her meeting with us immediately after the teacher left, but we paused her. Politely, we asked her why she wasn't aware of the meeting with that teacher and why she hadn't reviewed her calendar earlier that day. Had she done so, she would have noticed the conflict, communicated it, apologized for double-booking, and then sent the teacher new meeting time options.

Why didn't she do this, instead of having that very pregnant teacher walk all the way to her office? Even in the moment, she should have apologized, taken three minutes to find a new time, and even gotten up and walked the teacher out. Now the teacher was going to have to wait for the principal to "follow up with some suggested new times," which, by the way, the principal didn't make a note of, so there was no way of knowing if that was going to actually happen.

Too often, staff are in the dark about things that matter. A Monday email references a Thursday field trip that no one knows about; classroom visitors have been scheduled for weeks, but the teachers only find out about it that same morning; staff still have no specifics from leadership about their school's Spirit Week—that starts next week.

Recently, we were at a school where the location for a 1:00 p.m. meeting hadn't been shared. All the invitees were in different spaces, texting one another to find out where they needed to be. Mistakes happen. We acknowledge that. But that's not what we're talking about here. We're talking specifically about something else: about school leaders who don't believe that effective and efficient communication, delivered with plenty of time for people to take action, is important to their people. But it is.

Effective Communication

What It Is

Effective communication refers to clear, concise, transparent messaging about all things school related delivered by leaders to leaders, by leaders to teachers and school staff, and by leaders to families.

Why It Matters

A study of workplace communication (Fierce, Inc., 2011) found that 86 percent of employees attribute workplace failures to lack of collaboration and communication. But you don't need us to tell you that. Being in the dark, being surprised by things at work, and being under pressure because of last-minute asks are infuriating. It breaks down a culture as fast as anything in schools.

Best Practices for Planning

Effective communication in schools fosters collaboration, enhances student success, and strengthens relationships among administrators, teachers, students, parents, and the community. Consider the following best practices.

Use Multiple Communication Channels

Schools must intentionally use multiple channels of communication even in the face of redundancy. There is no such thing as overcommunication here. Both internal and external messages should be disseminated in three to five channels. We list several here:

- **Email and newsletters.** Share important updates, reminders, and event details.
- **School website and portals.** Maintain a central hub for school information, policies, and announcements.
- **Social media** (Facebook, Twitter, Instagram). Engage with parents and the community in real time.
- **Mobile apps and text messaging.** Provide quick updates and emergency notifications.
- **Printed materials.** Ensure accessibility for families with limited digital access.
- **Town halls and community meetings.** Encourage face-to-face engagement and Q&A sessions.

To be clear, we are *not* suggesting that you communicate directly with your team in myriad ways (e.g., you're texting one AP, emailing another, and stopping by a teacher's room, all while sending messages on Slack). This will lead to a mountain of communication that is likely to be ignored. What we are referring to here is the dissemination of need-to-know information.

Be Consistent in Your Messaging

Consistency is essential in terms of fostering a culture of healthy communication.

- **Be predictable.** Messages should arrive to their audiences on a consistent timeline (e.g., weekly newsletters, monthly town halls).
- **Be mindful of inbox overload.** Avoid sending one-off emails or messages unless they're time sensitive. Flooding staff members' email boxes with single tasks that just popped into your head can lead to confusion and ultimately disregarding.

- **Speak with one voice.** All school communication should align with the school vision, values, and goals, which should be visible in every written and verbal communication. Ensure that external and internal messaging are in a unified voice. Avoid mixed messages by coordinating communication across departments and leadership teams.

Encourage Two-Way Communication

Just telling staff members that you are open to feedback is insufficient. You'll need to create intentional and safe (that is, judgment- and consequence-free) opportunities for staff to voice concerns and ask questions. This will also be integral for students and families. Just think about all the times a family member simply showed up at your school wanting to speak with you. Formalizing how this looks will allow for less confusion, less frustration, and more time for you.

- **Survey stakeholders.** Frequently use surveys and polls to gather insights on school climate, communication effectiveness, and stakeholder needs. Provide opportunities for anonymous responses to ensure that every voice is included.
- **Be publicly available.** Hold open office hours or special events so parents and staff can meet with administrators. Some examples are Muffins for Moms and Doughnuts for Dads and Faculty Feedback Fridays.
- **Acknowledge inquiries and concerns.** Respond promptly to any communications from stakeholders. Even if you don't have the answer to their question, let them know when you'll get back to them. This builds trust and reinforces your commitment to openness and solutions-oriented leadership.
- **Choose the best communication process for urgent needs and asks.** Not everything in schools can be planned out in this way. Some days, a teacher may need to go home sick, so you need another adult in that area of the school. Whether it's an app, walkie-talkies, or text messages, choose *the* way that kind of communication should occur, and hold everyone accountable to communicating in that way.

Best Practices for Staff Rollout

The rollout for effective communication will look different from the rollouts we've discussed thus far. That's because it's less tangible and more of an idea. Sure, there will be actual strategies and potentially training around certain applications, but ensuring everyone knows that effective communication is something leadership is committed to and that, as a school, you're going to prioritize this, will look different. We offer a two-pronged approach: Leaders agree on a commitment to effective communication, and then they present it to staff.

Begin with Buy-In

Whether using survey data or research, you must get other leaders to buy into the importance of effective communication. They may need to reflect on areas where they're excelling and on areas where they can improve. It's important to note that some leaders may see this entire idea as a "whole lotta nothing." Just like someone who fails to motivate themself to go to the gym on a rainy day, they'll give themselves an out. You need to ensure that no one gets that out. This matters. The data are clear. The anecdotes are clear. You must be committed to this.

Share with Staff

Leaders need to publicly express a commitment to effectively communicating. Share examples of what this will look like when done well and what it will look like when done poorly.

For example, leaders may say, "You will have the daily briefing in your inbox by 6:30 a.m. every morning. We commit to that. We need you to commit to reading it before you start the work day, so please do not ask questions that were included in it." They might also say, "Unless it's urgent, we will not email you during the work day for anything. We want you to be able to focus on teaching."

Reiterate the importance for staff to effectively communicate with one another around student concerns, time-off requests, and missed deadlines. "This looks like sending one email if you have multiple asks or questions and not six. It looks like approaching a colleague and referencing our value of Team First if them being behind on deadlines is affecting your work."

Ask them to contact you and the team when the leaders' communication doesn't feel effective. If you continue to message that you want this feedback and if you act on it when you receive it, staff members will follow suit.

Best Practices for Execution

Keep in mind these best practices as you hone your communication skills.

Focus on Accessibility and Inclusiveness

All external communication should be translated into the known different languages in the school community. Be sure to use clear, jargon-free language.

Offer Multiple Formats

Include audio, visual, or written options if possible to ensure accessibility for all individuals. Leverage a school communication platform (e.g., Remind, ClassDojo, or Blackboard) to streamline messaging among teachers, students, and families. This will enable you to automate routine communications on a scheduled and recurring basis.

Do a Final Check

Does your school have a communication strategy that

- Prioritizes clarity and accessibility?
- Fosters engagement and two-way communication?
- Ensures consistency across all platforms?
- Aligns with school goals and values?

Considerations for Special Education

Schools must work to reject deficit-based language and narratives while reinforcing high expectations, as leader communication strongly shapes staff beliefs and instructional behavior (Ainscow et al., 2006; Kozleski et al., 2007). Avoid using language like "SPED student" or the "SPED department." Instead, model student-first, asset-based language when speaking about students with disabilities. Example language can include "students with learning differences," "student with an IEP or disability," and "Specialized Learning Department."

Anchor all communication, feedback, and accountability conversations in shared language, referencing the school vision and adult expectations when instruction, collaboration, or compliance for students with disabilities falls short (Fixsen et al., 2005). Regarding families, use clear, jargon-free communication and multiple access points, as family-school communication is a critical predictor of trust and student success (Blue-Banning et al., 2004).

As with all aspects of school communication systems, messaging regarding special education must be proactive, not reactive. Leaders must establish predictable routines for sharing student progress, instructional adjustments, and concerns before issues escalate (Billingsley et al., 2020).

Common Pitfalls to Avoid

We've alluded to some pitfalls throughout this chapter, but let's synthesize them here.

Not Communicating—About Communication

Effective communication can feel nebulous, with one person thinking they're communicating effectively and another disagreeing vehemently. You need to continually check in about how you're doing. You need to provide feedback about communication. Assuming you're all being clear is a formula for failure.

Thinking It's "Nice" but Not Necessary

Effective communication is not a "touchy-feely" thing that you leave behind when the heat gets turned up. If you put it off to "one day, when things have settled down," it will simply never happen. Address this issue *now.* It's not optional. Don't underestimate its crucial importance.

Not Ensuring People Are Receiving and Internalizing Your Communications

In schools, people tend to unintentionally "tell on themselves." This looks like someone asking you the answer to something that is clearly written in the weekly email or a one-pager at summer training (think back to our leadership playbook). In addition to repeatedly messaging that communication matters and that part of that is reviewing other people's communication, always hold people accountable to going back to the source. "That's in our weekly email. Please review it and reach back out if you have any questions." If this seems unkind, we invite you to think of it as incredibly kind, as you're setting this person up for success in the future by ensuring they'll read and internalize what they receive.

Some leaders have resorted to including "Easter eggs" in their emails to ensure they're being read (e.g., including a line partway through an email, "The first five people to email me their favorite color will get a Starbucks gift card"). Although we don't hate this idea and have seen examples of it working, it's better to rely on shared responsibility rather than tricks.

An Essential Conversation About Exemplifying Effective Communication

Questions to Keep in Mind

- What does "good" look like?
- Are people clear about that?
- Are people meeting that bar?
- Where are the gaps?
- What do I need to address immediately?

The Context: A teacher has failed to communicate with their peers around an upcoming event.

The Essential Conversation

"Hey, Mr. Phillips, can I provide you with a next step around your communication? Thanks. It's come to my attention that teachers found out about the field trip only two days before the event was scheduled to take place. As busy as we are, it's paramount that we're communicating with staff both early and often so they can prepare and so they feel we're valuing their time. Can you commit to that going forward? Can I support you in any way? Thanks so much."

PART II

Teaching and Coaching

6

Embrace and Model Explicit Instruction

No subject gets us in more trouble with school leaders and teachers, nor gives people more "aha" moments once their anger subsides, than the subject of instruction. Having spent significant time in hundreds of classrooms in U.S. cities (and internationally as well), we know that teachers are working extraordinarily hard. They're working before and after school. They're working weekends grading papers and planning lessons. In school, they're sharpening pencils, stopping nosebleeds, racing to get copies from oft-broken copy machines, waiting hours for bathroom breaks, and shoveling food into their faces during inhumanely short lunch breaks.

Being a teacher is as noble and as difficult a profession as there is. We admire and respect them. We also *were* both teachers: Antonio in North Philadelphia and Michael in South Philadelphia. Teachers are amazing humans who often spend more time with our children than we do.

The issue we have here is with the actual *teaching* itself—the explicit modeling of skills with clear and replicable steps, things that students can point to when it comes to how to annotate a novel for character traits, review a legal decision, or sound out a word they don't know.

In a math class, instead of explicitly modeling, a teacher will often ask students, "What do *you* think I do first?" This practice often elicits a handful of call-outs from the most confident students, some of whom share incorrect information, muddying the waters for the other students.

Or consider a story that Antonio recounts about an English teacher who asked students to read and summarize a short story. Totally absent from the room was an example of what a good summary looked like. There was no modeling; there were no anchor charts or exemplars on the board or in the worksheets for the kids to imitate. As you can imagine, every student's summary looked wildly different, with some kids attempting to rewrite the entire story, others writing down their impressions of the story, and some students actually doing an OK job of summarizing it.

There's an argument to be made, of course, for not spoon-feeding students, for having them figure out some things on their own. We agree. But not in the case we've just described. Summarizing is a relatively simple skill that leads students to master more advanced skills. It's not something they should have to "figure out" and do poorly as a result. The teacher should have explicitly taught this so that students could do it well.

A few years ago, Michael was in Atlanta, Georgia, and had the opportunity to participate in the Porsche Driving Experience. This is where someone gets to spin out (intentionally), ride the brake, and race different Porsche cars around a track. When the instructors met with Michael and his friends, they didn't let them behind the wheel without any training, they didn't ask them what *they thought* they should do first, and they didn't simply *talk* about Porsche cars and then end the experience.

No. With precise detail, they explained every aspect of the experience. They modeled step by step what it took to drive the cars. They showed videos. They even shared some pitfalls.

When Michael and his friends got into the cars, they had instructors with them who explained with impeccable clarity exactly what the drivers should do. They then coached and corrected the drivers throughout the process.

Explicit Instruction

What It Is

"Explaining every aspect," "modeling step by step," "coaching," and "correcting" are explicit instruction, and in the classroom, it looks very similar to Michael's Porsche experience. The teacher should share the day's objective (or the objective for that block) and then model how students should engage with that objective using a clear set of steps designed to lead to mastery.

Why It Matters

When learning new skills, explicit instruction plays a critical role in accelerating student learning. Research consistently demonstrates that clear modeling, guided practice, and structured direct instruction significantly improve students' understanding, retention, and ability to transfer knowledge to new contexts (Archer & Hughes, 2011; Hattie, 2009). By making cognitive processes visible and providing systematic scaffolding, explicit teaching practices reduce rote learning and support deep conceptual mastery.

Yes, yes, we know—promoting explicit instruction in a world of "student-centered instruction" can feel a bit counterintuitive. In fact, many educators have decided that explicit instruction no longer meets their students' needs. But as we say to people all the time, you don't get to blame the thing because you're bad at executing the thing. Explicit instruction works; it's the foundation for pushing students toward more and more rigorous work. Yet despite this, it's rarely done.

Best Practices for Planning

The first and arguably most important component to building teacher skill around explicit teaching is having leaders who believe it matters—and who feel comfortable messaging this to teachers. Let's be honest. Far too many leaders believe that what's happening in their teachers' classrooms is none of their business, and they have, intentionally or unintentionally, communicated this idea to teachers. Saying things like, "You know your students better than anyone" or "It's your kingdom in there. Just let me know if you need anything" will completely undermine your ability to improve your teachers.

You're the boss. Or one of the bosses. If you owned a restaurant, you'd have every right to change the menu. You'd have every right to give feedback to the waitstaff if they were running the food out too slowly. If you managed a car dealership, you'd be well within your role to tell staff how they should greet customers. You'd be totally in line with your responsibilities to set increasingly ambitious goals for sales in a given quarter.

Because that's the case, why do so many leaders abdicate their responsibility about what's actually happening in classrooms? There are a few reasons. The first is time. These leaders may not have the time because systems are lacking, calendars don't exist or aren't followed, or roles and responsibilities aren't defined. Or they simply may *think* they don't have the time, so they leave what's happening in classrooms solely to the teachers. They treat instruction as something that would be nice to focus on, but not as something they *must* focus on.

The second reason they leave instruction to the teachers is because they typically don't feel confident modeling what great teaching looks like. We know a lot of school leaders. They're amazing, caring people. But most weren't exemplary teachers, so they feel funny walking into classrooms, saying, "That's not working. It should look like this."

And the final reason is that they're worried that teachers won't be receptive to their feedback or, rather, their "meddling." A leader told us, "I don't want everyone to quit!" Although we see the point, we've never witnessed a school where half the teachers left because a system or approach changed.

If you're a leader who's mostly left instruction to the teachers, or to a few instructional coaches or an assistant principal, you'll need to have a much heavier hand here if you're going to influence what's happening in classrooms in the way we believe you should. Now maybe the idea of telling teachers that you're going to implement a new instructional approach, when you've mostly left them alone to teach in the way they see fit, will send chills down your spine. If so, skip this chapter, and come back to it when you're ready. If your school is missing a vision, if you rarely mention your values, if no one follows calendars, if your culture systems are broken—skip this, and get those pieces figured out first. And don't for one second feel bad about it. But do come back to this matter of instruction because you won't go far without it.

Where to Begin

Now for those of you who are still with us, the first thing you need to do is align your leadership team around the need for more explicit instruction. (See Figure 4.1 for a listing of possible leadership team members.) This will include presenting your rationale to them, collecting data on what's happening in classrooms (including how much actual teaching is occurring), and modeling explicit teaching for them.

We suggest you begin this modeling phase by teaching a lesson on a real-world skill, like throwing a curveball, doing tree pose in yoga, or baking an apple pie. Through this process, the steps for success will become abundantly clear. Soon, you'll be ready to plan and then model actual lessons for teachers.

Don't feel compelled to teach outside your expertise here. If you used to teach middle school writing, plodding your way through a chemistry lesson might not go too well. Teach your subject matter. Make sure to include a tangible, measurable objective—for example, "Students will be able to multiply three-digit numbers" or "Students will be able to assign personality traits to multiple characters within a text." After modeling several lessons, have other leaders do the same thing for your small group, first with a real-life skill and then with an actual lesson they've taught.

Do not skip the above. We're convinced that the six most powerful words in education, urban or otherwise, are, "Watch me model this for you." Because so few leaders do it. Because they're scared it won't go well.

But you're not them. So do it.

There's one other major piece to plan for. Many schools rely on curriculum or programming to save the day. However, those programs still need someone to train and coach the teachers in an ongoing way to ensure fidelity, and most schools don't provide much beyond the initial roll-out. To complicate the matter, a lot of these new programs have unique, to put it mildly, models that begin with the ending and ask students to work backward to figure out the steps themselves. They don't include clear steps for how students are going to master the content. Sometimes they're theoretical, with 5 to 10 different objectives, most of which aren't measurable (students will "understand" as opposed to "list") and that mostly muddy the waters for already overworked teachers.

However, the good news is that most of these programs are relatively easily modified to meet our criteria. Part of your planning should include modifying a handful of lessons so that when you roll out this idea to teachers, you can present concrete examples.

Finally—and this is crucial—you and your team need to agree on what good instruction looks like. Too often, leaders avoid classrooms because they're not quite sure what they're looking for. They might walk into a classroom to observe, stand there for a while, maybe take some notes, then not have all that much to say to the teacher afterward, except for generalities like, "It looked good in there."

Recently, we were at a school in the United Kingdom. Before entering the classrooms, we asked the leaders what "good" instruction looked like. All five of them had no idea. They responded with terms like "rigorous" and "student-centered," but they couldn't define what these things actually meant. When we got into various rooms, some students were sitting on top of their desks, some had no writing materials, and some teachers and teacher's assistants were off to the side, working one-on-one with students. This is not the whole-group, explicit instruction we're talking about here.

You can choose whatever model of explicit instruction that makes the most sense for you, or you can combine a few different ones. Or, yes, and we are biased here, you can head to https://skyrocketed.org/frameworks, download our Teacher Coaching Framework for free, and use as your baseline our Strand 2, which focuses on content mastery and includes 11 foundational teacher actions.

Please know that the only way you will ever maximize your potential as an instructional team or as a school is by having a crystal-clear vision of what good instruction looks like, ensuring that everyone understands it with impeccable clarity, training and retraining teachers around it, and aligning all your feedback to it.

Best Practices for Staff Rollout

Let's be honest. Some teachers are *not* going to like this. It will be hard for them to disagree with the approach because these strategies have been proven to work, but it will make their teaching harder because they'll have to flex different muscles. We've often seen teachers push back on genuinely good ideas, not because they're uncaring, but because they've been asked to figure out their jobs on their own for so long or because they went all in on an initiative a year or so before that ended up going away without a sound.

So lean on data here. Schoolwide data. National data. Data on the importance of explicit teaching. Roll out whatever your "good" is to teachers. Get them to see what the differences are between their current approaches and this new approach. Provide support around planning during the summer, and commit to planning with them during the year.

Maybe most important, teachers should know that they can count on you for ongoing support and coaching—and that you will hold them accountable. You will need to dedicate significant time to this. If you can't, maybe skip this one for now. Because just like a skydiver who pulls the cord and whose parachute only opens halfway, this is not something you can launch halfway.

Best Practices for Execution

And now's the time to execute. Consider these best practices.

Model the Steps

Every single lesson needs to meet the expectations that you and the other leaders have agreed to. Even if you start small—say, by asking teachers to post a measurable objective for every lesson and relay it to students—the expectations should be clear. The objectives might look like these:

- Students will be able to annotate the conflict in a text.
- Students will be able to identify the components of a chemical reaction.

Teachers then must provide students with the actual steps needed to master this content. The best way for them to do this is to engage in the exercise, do the work themselves, and then include the steps they took in those plans and in their model.

And what does that look like? It looks like the teacher up at the board, marker in hand, walking students through the process, piece by piece. Students will likely have pencils down at this point, with their attention solely on the teacher. The teacher can ask students to fill in some component after they've modeled a specific step, but they should get right back to the modeling afterward. Often, students are asked to take copious notes during this process. This is not a valuable use of time because it takes away from the instruction.

Recently, we observed an art teacher in Beloit, Wisconsin, teaching his class to make clay pots. He had all the scholars gather around, and with a clarity and step-by-step precision that every teacher would benefit from providing, showed students exactly how to make the pots. When it came to the lids, he showed the students how much glue to use, which direction to apply it from, how to place the lid on top, how many times to push it down, and how long they needed to hold it for it to stick. *This* is what this component of the lesson should look like.

Now, it's time to practice. First, the teacher should ask all students to complete step 1 or steps 1 and 2 of a given problem—say, annotating a specific paragraph. This work should be done on their own, with the teacher circulating, looking for trends and providing individual support. It's important, however, that teachers do not skip the model and then spend this time simply teaching the skills to a handful of students. Although reteaching is important, it should occur only after a model failed to land with certain students. Students also shouldn't be working with partners at this point. Working with a partner on something they barely know how to do will either lead to doing it wrong—because the other student did it wrong—or simply mask the fact that they didn't do the work because the other person did it for them. The teacher can have the partners share what they came up with but only *after* they've completed the requested steps.

Check for Understanding

As referenced above, during this component of the lesson, the teacher should be circulating the room, checking for understanding, seeing what the student work product looks like in relation to the model, and providing either individual or whole-group feedback. The teacher also should be checking for understanding in the independent practice that follows. Just to clarify, we mean *independent practice,* not group work. When we're teaching students something new, one student in the group may end up carrying the entire group.

Teachers should provide feedback after checking for understanding. It might sound like this:

- "Hey, steps 1 and 2 look really strong. Look at step 3 again. You missed something there."
- "Class, I want you to focus on step 4. You must choose one side in your argument. If you've chosen both sides, opt for one or the other and make that change."

In some cases, the teacher might need to reteach the content based on the data they collected. They may need to give more challenging work to students who easily mastered the lesson, and they may need to give extra support to students who struggled. The teacher should conclude the lesson by sharing student progress toward mastering the content. Students can also self-assess by means of an exit ticket. One way or the other, the students should be absolutely clear at the end of the lesson whether they mastered the objective that was posted earlier on.

Think back to the summary lesson that Antonio observed.

"OK, our objective today was to summarize this short story. Our steps were to include all character names, to share the inciting incident, to write at least one challenge the characters faced in resolving their conflict, and to share how the story resolved.

"I've circulated and we're a perfect 24 for 24 on steps 1, 3, and 4. We are 21 out of 24 for step 2, which is that inciting incident. Remember, the inciting incident is the pivotal event that disrupts a character's normal life and sets the conflict into motion. We'll continue working on this next week. Great work!"

Considerations for Special Education

Years ago, at a partner school in Los Angeles, a special education teacher pushed back on this idea of explicit instruction, citing the severity of her students' disabilities and their inability, in her mind, to be able to engage with explicit instruction. We asked her what that day's objective was.

"Students will be able to identify a nickel among a group of coins."

"OK," we asked her. "Tell us what happened in the lesson?"

"I held up a nickel and said, 'Who knows what this is?'"

She told us that of her five students, three knew right away. A fourth would have known, but he wasn't paying attention, and she said that the fifth likely wouldn't have known.

This teacher's objective was essentially a question that 80 percent of the students already had the answer to.

This doesn't speak to anyone's inability to master content that's taught explicitly. It speaks to the low bar she had for her students (this is not a judgment; she just needed coaching).

Students with special needs, like you, like us, and like your general education students, need to be explicitly taught. It might need to look a bit (or a lot) different, but they need it just the same.

Depending on your instructional model, schools should consider explicit instruction as a nonnegotiable expectation for students with disabilities. Instruction models with clearly defined core components (clear objectives, modeling, guided practice, checks for understanding) are supported by extensive research that shows explicit instruction significantly improves outcomes for students with learning and cognitive disabilities (Archer & Hughes, 2011; Hattie, 2012).

Another nonnegotiable is the alignment between IEP goals and explicit instructional practices, ensuring students receive research-based, systematic, and scaffolded instruction rather than an overreliance on discovery-based or unsupported approaches that may limit access to learning (McLeskey et al., 2014).

Instructional leadership teams will need to continuously monitor and model explicit instruction as leaders and coaches, demonstrating lessons and walkthrough "look-fors" so that teachers clearly understand what effective practice looks like in real classrooms, especially for diverse learners (Rosenshine, 2012). This whole-school team (not just special education) should monitor instructional fidelity and student response by using progress monitoring systems, multi-tiered systems of supports (MTSS), and IEP data to ensure explicit instruction is delivered consistently and adjusted based on student need (Gersten et al., 2009).

Work to find concrete ways to integrate explicit instruction into coaching, feedback, and evaluation systems, using shared language and evidence-based criteria to address inconsistencies in implementation for students with disabilities (Fixsen et al., 2005).

Common Pitfalls to Avoid

We're losing millions of hours of instructional time every year. If you multiply 180 school days by 8 hours, you get 1,440 hours. If a school has 1,000 students, that's almost a million and a half total school hours in one year. Now some of that time is taken up by necessary lunches or assemblies or transitions. But most of it is instructional time (or it should be). Let's say, however, that 25 percent of that instructional time—and we promise you, it's *way* higher than that—has students in workbooks, in groups discussing things they're not prepared to discuss and haven't been taught, and overall "doing things" like following along or writing summaries they don't know how to write, as opposed to "learning things" through explicit instruction. We are losing thousands and thousands of hours of instructional time per school. Across a district, the number is staggering. Across an entire city, it's unfathomable. As such, you can likely see why we're not writing about restorative justice in this book.

As a school leader who's committed to explicit instruction, you must keep an eye out for the following pitfalls.

Lowering the Bar

Asking students to complete page 19 in a workbook is easy. What we're describing here is hard. Explicitly modeling skills every day, during every block, will take time, patience, and persistence. Teachers will get frustrated. You may get frustrated. The students? They probably won't get frustrated at all because they will have a newfound clarity to guide them.

If a teacher is struggling mightily at first, modify what you're asking of them. You might stipulate in the beginning that they only need to explicitly model in math or only on specific days of the week. Although it's not great for students to sometimes be on the receiving end of great teaching and sometimes not, we're building toward more consistency, and it's probably OK. What's *not* OK is for teachers to suggest that this is too hard to execute and for you to accept that. Teachers are smart. They know lots of things in schools simply go away. As a colleague of ours says, "They wait us out." Modifications and differentiation are OK. Lowering the bar and not holding people accountable will *ensure* it goes away.

Blaming Students

Another major pitfall here is accepting a teacher's negative perceptions of their students as being the reality. Sometimes, teachers who aren't practiced in the kind of explicit instruction we're describing may resort to blaming students for their own misses. For example, a teacher may be faced with a number of kids who didn't understand the lesson. This teacher has a choice: They can evaluate where the gaps in their own teaching were, revise their materials, and reteach it. Or they can say, "The kids didn't get it" or "It's too hard for them" or "They're not ready for this." From our experience, they often do the latter. Not because they don't care, but because they genuinely don't know how to do it better. That's where you come in.

Failing to Plan

Michael used to work with a physics teacher who would show up 10 minutes before the first bell, without anything planned for students, often walking into class at the same time as they did. He would welcome students and after settling them down, would simply write an equation on the board. He'd sit on top of his desk as they spent the entire class time discussing it. This isn't teaching. At least not how we're describing it. And it's not what kids in our cities need.

Planning is imperative in a model like this. And planning takes time—to ensure the lesson includes measurable objectives, steps for success, and explicit models. It takes time to ensure that what the teacher wrote down in their plans is *actually* being taught. So it's important that even when things get tough, which they will, that you still hold your teachers accountable for exemplar planning, that you're actively reviewing and providing feedback on what they submit, and that you're in classrooms providing feedback.

Fearing to Look Foolish

Standing in front of people, whether it's 10 or 10,000, can be scary. What's scarier still is telling them, "Stop what you're doing, and watch me. Watch me teach you how to do this thing."

The fact is, people are typically afraid that they won't actually be able to teach us. This is why so much professional development and teaching in general miss the mark: People just don't want to look foolish. They do lots of different things in front of us, but they rarely say, "Watch every move I make right now. This is going to make you better."

We see this play out with teacher coaches *all the time.* We spend hours with them analyzing the data from a teacher's class, scripting out glows and grows, and designing a practice session that requires the coach to model a skill for the teacher. Then we all pack into the teacher's room to observe the coaching session. When it gets to the practice portion, however, the coach often steers the conversation away from the model or lets the teacher pull them off course. Either way, they never get to the part where the coach shows the teacher what "good" looks like.

Understand that your teachers will do this in front of students as well, not because they don't care, but because modeling a lesson may be difficult for them, and they'll be nervous. Collect data on these instances. Share the data with teachers. And show compassion here. The teacher likely just needs more practice, which is what our essential conversation template means to address.

An Essential Conversation About Embracing and Modeling Explicit Instruction

Questions to Keep in Mind

- What does "good" look like?
- Are people clear about that?
- Are people meeting that bar?
- Where are the gaps?
- What do I need to address immediately?

The Context: A teacher is unwilling to use explicit instruction in their classroom.

The Essential Conversation

"Hi, Ms. Lewis, can I share some feedback? I read the email you sent me about you not believing that explicit instruction was best for your students. I appreciate, as always, your contributions, so thank you. However, I've shared the research, the data, as well as the rationale around this move. So although it may not feel like it's working just yet, I'm asking that you stick with it, with my support, and that you continue trying. Our vision, in part, talks about preparing our students for high school. Part of that is ensuring they have the academic skills to move seamlessly from our school to their next stop. I believe you're absolutely the right person to do that for them as it pertains to math. So can you commit to continuing to try this approach with my support?"

Our Rationale

Of course, the teacher could say no here. At that point, you might need to document their response as insubordination. But remember, this teacher is likely scared because they're out of their comfort zone. It makes more sense to ferret out the root cause of their concerns and address them. The teacher probably needs compassion, more training, and more support—and not punishment.

7

Engage in Instructional Coaching

When Michael started Skyrocket Education, he had one purpose: to teach school leaders how to coach teachers in an intentional, structured, step-by-step way. For too long and in too many schools, he observed instructional leaders walking through the halls unsure of themselves, grabbing photocopies for teachers, sharing resources—and making very little difference in terms of actual classroom instruction.

Too many people charged with driving instruction in their schools—in this chapter we'll refer to them as "coaches," but we mean you and your team—have become "friendly helpers." They walk up to a teacher's door, sheepishly knock as the teacher is grading papers, and ask, "Is there anything you need?" Teachers either respond no because they don't feel like the friendly helper can do anything for them ("no" doesn't mean everything is perfect; it's a school after all) or "Yeah, do you have any resources for teaching the main idea?"

The coach is thrilled to be of service, so they flip open their computer and email some resources to a teacher who may or may not use them. Then the coach exits, hoping their resources will be helpful—and hoping they didn't disturb the teacher too much.

We've seen this. *You've* seen this. This is *not* coaching. Too many coaching and instructional "experts" assume that getting teachers to a place of being highly effective is like trying to answer a confusing, ambiguous riddle. But it's not. We've worked in hundreds of schools globally, and the challenges in classrooms everywhere are staggeringly similar.

Still, some coaching models position coaches as the keepers of secret information that can only be unlocked if teachers answer the coach's "probing" questions perfectly. The teachers are required to navigate elaborate psychological mazes if they want to improve. This is an exhausting, patronizing waste of time.

We need coaches to be experts. Like Beyoncé, who's an expert at singing. Like Katie Ledecky, who's an expert at swimming. Like Daniel Day-Lewis, who's an expert at acting. Imagine you were lucky enough to receive tennis lessons from Serena Williams. It would be so invigorating to be taught by an expert. It'd be thrilling to know that in a short time, you'd be better because of her expert coaching.

Instructional Coaching

What It Is

It's a clear and precise teacher coaching model, grounded in data and education best practices, that is executed by expert coaches who set goals with teachers, designate specific actions for them to work on, model those actions, and have them practice those actions repeatedly. The sole purpose is to be better for students.

Why It Matters

Great schools coach their teachers. Period. This is particularly important to do in urban schools, where graduating is not a given and where so many lives are at stake. In the schools we work in—in the schools *you* work in—every single instructional minute matters. Some of you may have lost teachers midyear. You may have lost some in the first few weeks of school. You may even have had teachers show up one day and fail to appear the next.

Our city schools cannot afford to lose teachers because they're too stressed and undersupported. The best strategy for holding on to these teachers *and* elevating instruction and classroom culture is teacher coaching.

Best Practices for Planning

Instructional coaching is by far one of the most powerful tools for improving teaching practices, supporting professional growth, and ultimately enhancing student outcomes. Teacher coaching is not just a professional development tool; in fact, it is a key component of educational excellence and student achievement. When properly executed, it leads to better student outcomes, increased teacher satisfaction and retention, and a stronger school community.

Establish a Clear Vision for Coaching

Successful school leaders lead instructional coaching programs that begin with a clear purpose and structure and that are aligned with the school's or district's vision of instructional goals. This might sound like, *We believe every one of us can improve in meaningful ways through data collection, feedback, and coaching. It's what we deserve and it's what our staff, students, and families deserve.*

Once you've established this, then make sure to do the following:

- Define all the components of coaching, as well as the role of the coaches.
- Differentiate the coach's role in developing teachers from other support mechanisms, such as mentoring and professional development. A mentor teacher is the friendly helper we described earlier. They're usually a veteran teacher who teaches the same content as the teacher they're mentoring. They share resources and they're a person to lean on, but they don't make a teacher significantly better through hyper-focused coaching and intentional practice. Professional development, although helpful in developing the whole group,

is a beginning. It's usually too generalized to make any one teacher exceptional, though it does benefit the group when done well.

- Revisit the coaching vision with other leaders to ensure clarity and engagement.

Build Strong, Trusting Relationships

The best coaching relationships thrive on trust and mutual respect between teachers and coaches. In the absence of these, teachers may view coaching as punitive rather than developmental. Never use coaching as a tool to exit a teacher. If a teacher is underperforming, only provide coaching in an authentic effort to improve the teacher's practice. If they don't rise to the occasion, do what needs to be done. But coach them authentically.

Be sure to do the following:

- Discuss what communication in the coaching relationship will look like. Define what information will and will not be shared with other leaders. We recommend an open sharing of data and progress with personal matters to be shared if agreed upon. For instance, it should be no secret that Mr. Jennings is working on classroom culture and has an average of 67 percent of students on task throughout his lessons. It should be shared with other leaders that his goal is 85 percent eight weeks from now and that you are working on directions, scanning, and positive praise. However, if Mr. Jennings has an ill family member and asks you not to share that with anyone, don't. If he's stressed out and thinking about quitting, tell him you're compelled to share that with others, so you can support him.
- Provide a clear rationale as to why the teacher is receiving coaching. Clarify what you hope the coaching relationship will accomplish. Anchor these pieces in your vision and lived values. Ideally, you have something around improvement, being your best for students, and you're all lifelong learners. It's not unusual for teachers to see this as a punishment or a reflection of their poor performance. As you can't possibly coach everyone at once, think about including some more advanced teachers in an early cycle to dispel this belief.
- Informally check in with the teacher, and spend the time needed to build rapport before formal coaching begins. Share about yourself.

Ask about them. Talk about why you do what you do. Ask why they do. It's hard to coach people to be authentic, but authenticity is a must here. Eliminate distractions, make eye contact, ask questions, and speak about yourself less than you listen to them to cultivate this.

Create a Structured Coaching Cycle

A structured, concise, and easy-to-follow coaching cycle will provide a clear and consistent framework for supporting teachers in implementing new strategies. It typically should have three components:

1. **Pre-observation discussion.** In this brief meeting, the coach asks the teacher about their strengths, growth areas, and what they aspire to achieve as an instructor. It's important to note that in our model, the coach is the driver of the change and the decider of what to do first, next, last, and so on. What a teacher shares may not be what the coach determines the teacher needs to work on. Still, it's important to know if a teacher thinks they're great at writing higher-order questions even if they're not (as determined by observations), so the coach can soften the message when sharing what they're going to work on.
2. **Classroom observation.** The coach gathers data through direct and live observations or video recordings to determine baseline data and starting points. At the beginning of a cycle, the coach and teacher will likely look to achieve mastery on one student outcome goal (e.g., on task percentage or content mastery percentage) called the end-of-cycle big goal and a handful of specific teacher skills to get them there.
3. **Coaching meeting.** The coach provides specific, actionable feedback, rooted in data; names next steps for the teacher; and then engages them in a rigorous practice session designed to make them better right away. The coach shares next steps and goals for teacher and student success.

The coach should focus on one improvement area at a time (all driving toward the end-of-cycle big goal) to avoid overwhelming teachers. Video review can be used when in-person observation is not possible.

This can give space for the teachers to reflect on their own teaching as well.

Best Practices for Staff Rollout

Launching an effective instructional coaching program requires careful and thoughtful planning. Consider the following steps as you prepare to roll out a coaching program.

Define the Purpose and Goals

You will already have developed a vision statement for the instructional coaching program that will clarify why the coaching program is important and why it's being implemented. Providing a clear and justifiable rationale is imperative for staff buy-in.

- Designate specific instructional goals you're looking to achieve—for example, improving student engagement, strengthening differentiated instruction, or enhancing data-driven teaching.
- Script how coaching aligns with the school and district vision, values, and strategic priorities.
- Practice framing coaching as a support system rather than as an evaluative tool.
- Match coaches and teachers. You likely won't be able to coach everyone unless you have eight teachers. Think, instead, about how many can you coach effectively? You may personally coach only one teacher at a time. An AP may coach two. An instructional coach may coach seven. But again, think depth over breadth.

Share with Teachers

Effective communication is key to gaining teacher buy-in. Your teachers will need to see coaching as a valuable, nonthreatening opportunity for professional growth. To that end, follow these steps:

1. At a PD session, debut your instructional coaching kickoff program. Explain the purpose, process, and benefits of coaching. You will have already scripted these pieces in the previous step.

2. Address common concerns around time commitments, practice hesitancy, and the role of administrators in the process.
3. Highlight positive teacher testimonials, case studies, or research-based evidence in support of instructional coaching.

Initial Observations

You've shared your plan with teachers, and your coaches have had their pre-observation discussions. Now it's time to conduct the initial observation.

1. Inform teachers that you will be conducting initial classroom visits to launch the instructional coaching initiative.
2. Have coaches schedule a time that works to observe the teacher and for the subsequent feedback meeting.
3. Have coaches clarify that they will begin by collecting data that include objective, factual information free from personal opinions or judgments and that are directly aligned with the school's vision for instructional and classroom effectiveness. This first observation should be relatively long (30–40 minutes) to ensure you're getting a holistic view of the teacher's skillset.

Use the template shown in Figure 7.1 to discuss the initial observation. A full sample conversation on this topic can be found at the end of this chapter, in the Essential Conversation section (see Figure 7.3).

Best Practices for Execution

Once your coaching plan is ready for execution, the following practices will help ensure a long-lasting positive effect on your teacher development and student success.

Use Data-Driven Coaching

Using data to drive your coaching ensures that your instructional feedback and decisions are objective, are based on measurable goals, and are student centered. It removes perceptions of bias or judgment. Instead of saying, "Your class seemed out of control," which is a judgment call, it's preferable to say, "Twelve out of 23 students were out of their seats and

Figure 7.1
Initial Coaching Meeting Agenda

Step	Description
Frame the meeting agenda.	Conduct a personal check-in. "Here's what you can expect from this meeting and from future coaching meetings. . . ." Share that practice will occur.
Share glows and grows.	Share data, and explain your analysis and recommendations.
Share sound bite and teacher actions.	Share the big picture and possible solutions.
Reflect and invite feedback.	Ask for any context—that is, "their story." Ask them to reflect on the data, suggested teacher actions, and so on.
Practice.	This is the majority of the meeting—active skill building around the growth area.
Set goals.	Set targets around what will be different in both teacher and student performance one week from today.
Clarify next steps.	Put the next meeting and observations on the calendar. Discuss what will occur, specific to real-time coaching, in the next meeting.

not following your directions at 9:13 this morning." The low-inference nature of the data keeps personal feelings, judgment, and bias out of the equation. One study (Kraft et al., 2018) found that teachers who received data-informed coaching showed greater improvements in instructional effectiveness than those who received general feedback and development alone. Here are some additional pointers:

- Include metrics around student achievement and engagement, as well as data from classroom observations, to create a holistic view. Use these data to create a *sound bite,* a one-sentence description of exactly what's happening in the classroom right now. It includes both teacher actions and student outcomes and the causal relationship between them (e.g., "Students are not making significant progress toward mastering the objective because the teacher is not succinctly and efficiently modeling the precise steps and cognitive processes students are expected to take to master content").

- Set weekly teacher action goals (TAGs) and weekly student outcome goals (SOGs) all driving at the end-of-cycle big goal.
- Have teachers watch video recordings of exemplar lessons or record themselves teaching a lesson. Reviewing such recordings can facilitate reflective coaching discussions.

Model Effective Teaching

Teachers can benefit significantly from observing instructional strategies that are modeled in real classroom contexts. The research is clear that professional learning systems that include an instructional framework, explicit modeling, opportunities for guided practice, and focused feedback are far more effective at changing classroom practice than generic or unstructured support (Darling-Hammond et al., 2017; Yoon et al., 2021). These elements reflect the core features of high-impact professional development that supports teacher learning and instructional improvement. When leaders build coaching cycles that intentionally integrate these components, teachers will be better equipped to implement and sustain effective instructional strategies. It's advisable to do the following:

- Adopt a teacher coaching model and framework to standardize what model teaching looks and sounds like in your classrooms.
- Include modeling in coaching sessions, as well as opportunities for modeling in the classroom to showcase effective instructional strategies.
- Have instructional coaches co-teach with teachers to guide them through implementing new practices.

Provide Actionable Feedback (Sometimes in Real Time!)

Coaches' feedback to teachers should always be timely, specific, and focused on growth rather than just on identifying problems. General feedback like "You need to give better directions" is unclear and unactionable. Instead, the feedback should sound like this: "When giving directions, be sure to include four components: (1) the task (what students are expected to do); (2) the timing (how much time students have to complete the task); (3) materials (what students need to complete the task); and (4) the sound level at which students should complete the task." Coaches should use objective, nonjudgmental language when giving feedback, which is rooted in the data and in next steps.

Offer real-time, immediate feedback, particularly feedback "in the moment" when the teacher is actually teaching. That is a major driver of teacher development. It can build confidence (when the feedback is positive) and drive change (when it's constructive).

Considerations for Special Education

All too often, special education teachers are left out of coaching cycles. In many cases, they teach far fewer students, so they're sometimes deprioritized while the general education teachers are coached.

We understand that schools need to achieve tangible results on state assessments. Love them or loathe them, we often share that results on state tests keep the lights on. So yes, coaching teachers who teach the most students makes sense. But remember your vision. Remember your values. Remember, hopefully, that you're there for every student.

Find a way to coach special education teachers. They deserve it, and their students deserve it.

The next four chapters are specific to teacher coaching. We won't include special education considerations in them as we're asking you to think of the coaching in those chapters as relevant for all teachers, special ed or otherwise.

Common Pitfalls to Avoid

Although instructional coaching can significantly improve teaching effectiveness and student outcomes, many schools face challenges in implementation. Here are common pitfalls we've seen schools encounter when rolling out an instructional coaching program, as well as some suggestions for avoiding them.

Lack of Clear Purpose and Goals

When schools launch a coaching program with no specific objectives, teachers and administrators are unclear of its aims. Another stumbling block occurs when instructional coaching is introduced as a generic professional development initiative rather than as a targeted coaching and support system.

You need to define and communicate clear coaching goals aligned with the school vision and priorities. Develop a coaching vision statement to guide program implementation, and communicate the purpose of coaching to teachers and staff, emphasizing that it is nonevaluative and supportive.

Lack of Buy-In from Teachers

Teachers can perceive coaching as a top-down directive or as a form of evaluation, rather than as an opportunity to improve practice and growth. Some educators may resist coaching because they assume it's only for struggling or new teachers. Some leaders may worry that direct coaching will negatively affect their relationships with staff. A lack of transparency about how coaching will work can also lead to skepticism and fear.

You will need to frame coaching as a partnership. The coach will explicitly tell teachers what to do, but what's driving the work are the data gathered, the shared coaching framework, and the collaborative work. Create a culture of coaching by signaling that everyone gets a coach—even leaders. Be sure to provide all processes and policies about coaching, including all related documents, tracking, and data outputs.

Lack of Communication

When school leadership fails to explain what coaching looks like in practice—for example, they fail to describe coaching cycles or observation expectations—it can lead to confusion, loss of trust, and reluctance to participate.

A staff kickoff meeting, as we noted earlier, goes a long way toward explaining the coaching process, expectations, and benefits. Provide clear documentation (including frequently asked questions and a coaching overview) that outlines what teachers can expect with instructional coaching. Find a cadre of teachers who have experienced coaching to share their success stories with others. Just ensure you know what they're going to say first. A teacher sharing, "Yeah, I thought it'd be annoying, and it kind of was, but I toughed it out, and I think I see some improvements from it" won't do you much good.

Lack of Follow-Up and Accountability

A major pitfall awaits the leader who thinks of coaching sessions as one-time events, with no follow-up or sustained teacher support. This is a sure way to erode confidence in any coaching program. Implement a clear, concise, and structured coaching cycle (e.g., pre-meeting → goal setting → observation → post-observation feedback → repeat). Share the most pertinent data collected during classroom visits to track teacher progress toward goals. Hold regular feedback and coaching meetings to collect feedback from teachers and analyze student performance data.

Two Conversations About Instructional Coaching

In this section, we're pivoting from the format we've used up to now because this chapter demands something more structured. We'll look at two conversations here, which we'll present in the figures that follow.

Two Essential Conversations About Engaging in Instructional Coaching

Questions to Keep in Mind

- What does "good" look like?
- Are people clear about that?
- Are people meeting that bar?
- Where are the gaps?
- What do I need to address immediately?

Figure 7.2 shows guidelines for an essential conversation that an instructional coach might have with a teacher before they begin coaching. Figure 7.3 shows a conversation that might take place during the rollout coaching meeting.

Figure 7.2

Teacher Coaching Agenda: An Essential Conversation

Before Coaching Begins

- Introductions (5 minutes): "Who are you? Where are you from? What do you like to do on the weekends?" Share the same about you.
- Frame the meeting (2 minutes): "Today, I'd love to get to know you, share a bit about me, hear about your teaching, talk about the work we'll do in this cycle, and together we'll set some expectations for our coaching relationship."
- Questions (4 minutes): "Tell me about your teaching? What are you good at? Where can you grow? What are you hoping to get out of coaching?"
- Share your approach/model (3 minutes): Share the framework. Talk about data, direct feedback, practice, and real-time coaching. Let them know that there will be multiple classroom observations and meetings each week. Clarify that this is all in service of being amazing for students. Explain that (Skyrocket) coaching is intense. Ask for their feedback here: "What do you find exciting? What concerns do you have?"
- Expectations (6 minutes): Share your coaching expectations (see below). "Do you have additional concerns you'd like to add? Are you willing to agree to these expectations? If so, are you willing to hold me accountable for meeting them as well?"
- Share contact information (2 minutes): Share email addresses and phone numbers. Let them know they can call, text, or email you if they need anything.
- Next steps (3 minutes): Put your first observation and your next meeting with them on the calendar. If there's anything you need them to send you, such as routine scripts, objectives, and so on, set those deadlines here.
- Thank them (1 minute): Show genuine excitement at the opportunity to work with them.

Coaching Expectations

1. Arrive on time.
2. Bring your framework/teaching standards and any assigned prework.
3. Submit deliverables on time.
4. Strive for solutions.
5. Focus on students.
6. Embrace practice.
7. Overcommunicate (concerning lateness, responding to emails within 24 hours, etc.).

Figure 7.3

Example of the Initial Coaching Meeting

Step	Sample Conversation
Frame the meeting agenda: • "Here's what you can expect from this meeting and from future coach-ing meetings. . . ."	"Good morning, Ms. G. Thank you so much for having me in your room on Tuesday. It was great to see you at work. What we're going to do today is review the notes and data that I took down, talk about your big-picture glows and grows, identify the most important action steps, set some goals, and land on any next steps. This meeting will look a bit different from our normal coaching meetings. Today we'll mostly be reviewing our coaching plan, whereas our future meetings will focus more on practicing specific skills, setting weekly goals, and identifying real-time coaching strategies to use. That meeting will take place at the same time each week. We'll set that time at the end of this meeting. Are you ready to dive in?" Make sure to check in with the teacher before you dive into this script. A simple "How was your weekend?" usually gets the job done.
Share glows and grows: • Share data, and explain your analysis and recommendations.	**Glows:** "You have some really efficient routines and proce-dures that create student leadership. For example, three stu-dents went to the bathroom during the class and were given passes by your bathroom pass coordinator, and there was no disruption to instruction. Awesome! "Also, when you redirected students to meet your expec-tations, you did so using student-friendly language, and students met your expectations. For example, at 10:42, you said, 'I need all laptops closed,' and 13 of the 15 students did so. You then said, 'I'm still waiting on two friends,' and both those students then closed their laptops at 10:43.' "Does that resonate with you? Are those things that you do intentionally?" **Grows:** "Not all the students are following class routines. For example, students were given 10 minutes to complete the two Do Now questions on their laptops; 9 of 15 students did so on time as 5 minutes were spent opening laptops, logging in, navigating tech issues, and so on. You didn't offer support for students during this time.

Step	Sample Conversation
	"Redirecting students was inconsistent. For example, at 10:51, five students had their heads down while you were teaching, and they were not redirected. At 10:54, three students were on their phones texting, and two others had their earbuds in. No redirection occurred. "What I'm noticing here is this: When you see students not meeting expectations, you redirect them, but you're not always seeing them."
Share sound bite and goals: • Share the big picture and possible solutions.	"The big picture here for us is that students are not on task throughout the lesson because you're not scanning the room after each direction to see that they're meeting the expectations. That's 1.8 on our framework. Please take a moment to read that. Overall, 61 percent of your students were on task. "You do have a strong foundation, and there were times when 87 percent of students were on task. I'm thinking that given where you are right now, by the end of our eight weeks together, you should have 95 percent of students on task. I'd like to make that our end-of-cycle goal. We'll start by focusing on scanning and go forward from there."
Reflect and invite feedback: • Ask for any context—that is, for "their story." • Ask them to reflect on the data, goals, and so on.	"I'd love to hear your thoughts. How do these notes and data points speak to you? How do you feel about the goals? Is there anything I should know? What questions do you have?"
Clarify next steps: • Put the next meeting and observations on the calendar. • Discuss what will occur, specific to real-time coaching, in the next meeting.	"OK, let's set our next meeting time. You have prep during 1st and 7th periods. Which period would you prefer to have our regularly scheduled coaching meeting? And what day of the week works best for you? "At our next meeting, we'll dive into practice around scanning the classroom to check for off-task behavior. Thank you so much for your time today. I can't wait to really dive in with you!"

8

Collect and Share Data

We once worked with an executive director in Cincinnati, Ohio, who, when a member of her team said that a teacher was doing better, asked them, "What does 'better' mean?" And when someone noted that a leader was struggling, she'd say, "What does 'struggling' mean?" But it wasn't always like this for this leader. In the past, when hearing such qualifiers as "better," "improving," "making changes," "not executing," and so on, she would simply move on.

This is a common trend in schools. For a field where numbers, growth, and measurement are so present in so many places, we use a staggeringly small amount of data in interactions on a day-to-day basis, especially when it comes to teaching and learning. And although, from our experience, the practice of collecting and meticulously analyzing and using data is pretty prevalent in urban schools—because there *is* such a focus on improvement—it still doesn't happen nearly enough.

This chapter is specific to data collection in teacher's classrooms. You can and should be collecting data on all things schoolwide—from student and staff tardies and absences, to lesson plan submissions, to level 2 and level 3 infractions, to benchmark and state assessments, and everything in between. Data are collected and shared schoolwide as an opportunity for celebration and to target areas for growth. We'll write more about this in Chapter 19.

Data Collection

What It Is

Data collection, specific to teaching, is about collecting information about both teacher actions and their corresponding student outcomes. It is an unbiased, cut-and-dried approach that removes feeling and emotion from the work and focuses only on the facts.

Why It Matters

Collecting and sharing precise data enable incredibly busy teachers to pause and celebrate some wins. It also enables teachers and coaches to see, without judgment or bias, exactly what the truth of the work is. Coaches can then do a better job of looking at the objective numbers to determine what their next steps with teachers should be.

Best Practices for Planning

Here are some planning best practices as they pertain to collecting data.

Know What You're Looking For

Meaningful data are almost impossible to collect without a vision of what success should look like. These pieces can take the form of tangible goals from an internalized framework. Ultimately, they must be things that you agree are necessary in schools like teachers designing effective routines, sharing the steps for success, students being on task, students mastering content, and students deeply engaging with content. Knowing what you care about enables you to ask questions of yourself that sound like, "Did I count the number of call-outs in that observation? Handing in homework took six minutes. Should it take that long? Did I count how many students wrote down something in the 15 minutes we were in there? What are the exit ticket data telling me?"

Choose Your Tool

In reality, you can use any tool you're comfortable with to collect data. We're big fans of pen and paper, but we understand that's a bit antiquated. If you're going to use something more formal than that, ensure all leaders are using the same tool. Also, make sure it's aligned to whatever evaluation or coaching rubrics or frameworks you're using. Sometimes leaders use different tools to measure different data, and sometimes leaders on the same team all use different tools. This leads to confusion and frustration. Alignment and expediency are key here.

Years ago, we worked with a leader who wrote everything down with pen and paper. Then, later that day, they would spend hours updating the data into the school's shared tool. This may feel very thorough, but it's a major waste of time.

Make a Plan to Share Your Data

We're big fans of publicly sharing data. You may not be a fan yourself, especially if this is new for you, but understand that data sharing needs to occur. You might do this in leadership team meetings, with only a few people privy to the data, in which case whole-school data and individual teacher and student data can and should be shared. "Our average of classrooms with posted objectives is 93 percent with only Ms. Greene, Mr. Kaminsky, and Mr. Ferrell not consistently posting them."

Or you might share it at the beginning of every staff meeting or in weekly emails for everyone to see. Here, you should be less likely to share individual teacher's data but should opt for the broader number approach. Both of us taught in schools where teacher data were public, but only for the state assessments and benchmark exams. So not, "Mr. Sonbert hasn't turned in his lesson plans in three weeks, everyone. What a punk." Don't do that.

The idea is that you need to create a plan to share the data that you and your teams collect, individually with the teachers you're coaching, the teachers you've observed, and the whole school.

If we told you that we had found a new route for you to take to get to school—a route you were totally unfamiliar with—that could be faster than your current route, would you take it? Probably not. You'd have to change everything you knew about getting to school for a potential gain. But what if *we promised* the route was better? Like really, really promised? "I like my way," you might say. "It's the way I know."

But what if we told you that it'd save you 10 minutes each way every day? That's 100 extra minutes a week to read, go to the gym, play with your kids, or just veg out.

Well, this is exactly what's happening in schools. To get people on board for taking the new route, you need data to drive that change.

Best Practices for Staff Rollout

Consider the following practices.

Share Examples and Nonexamples of Feedback

Instead of "I really liked your pacing today" (nonexample), say, "For each of the six questions you asked during the time I was in the room, 24 of the 25 students began working within 10 seconds of you saying, 'Go,' with the 25th student, Mario, beginning 15 seconds after that. He did so mostly after you praised three students who were already working. One example is 'Grace, thank you for getting started right away and for working so hard.'" Teachers will immediately get what makes this approach better than what you're currently doing. Frame this push for more precise data as less personal and potentially less biased than what's happening now. This approach is not about what you *think* is happening. It's about what *is* happening objectively, as it pertains to the metrics of success in your school. Some teachers may push back. If you say, "I sampled six students and asked what the day's objective is, and two of six could tell me. They were Daysha and Paul. But Monica, Terry, Saeed, and Ryan couldn't," you might hear, "Monica hasn't been here all week, and Ryan never pays attention."

It's important how you respond here. Monica not being here all week would have nothing to do with whether or not she knew *that* day's objective. And if you say you're a school who cares about all kids, which you should, it's the teacher's *job* to *get* Ryan to pay attention. Still, even when context is provided, the data are the data. If Ryan isn't paying attention because of a serious personal matter, of course take that into consideration. But only if you and the teacher agree that, for a short period of time, it's safer and healthier for Ryan to be in school and not engaged than not in school at all.

Base Feedback on Facts

Teachers deserve feedback based on facts, not feelings. Share what data will be tracked initially and how those data will be shared. Tell them what they can expect from you and when this initiative will begin. Model what this portion of a feedback meeting might sound like. Seeing and hearing it will help prepare them for the real thing.

Best Practices for Execution

Let's focus now on what students and teachers are doing in classrooms. When you're observing a teacher, the first thing to do is count the number of students in the room. That number—say, 26—becomes the denominator in all the data you're going to collect going forward. If 14 of the 26 students begin working within 30 seconds of the teacher giving directions, our data show 14 out of 26. And those are good data to have. Even if those data aren't "good."

In our model, we collect data on three strands.

Strand 1: Time on Task

In this first strand, we're looking at *time on task*. That is, are the kids doing what the teacher is asking? And are they doing it in a timely manner? We once observed a classroom where overall on-task behavior was 100 percent. Now that was good. But it was taking the kids between one and three minutes to even get started. A two-minute task would take at least five minutes to complete. So, although the on-task overall number was high, it wasn't high *throughout* the lesson, and it certainly wasn't high as students began each task. These were important data to collect.

Strand 2: Progress Toward Content Mastery

In this second strand, we're looking at *progress toward content mastery*. We're still counting the number of students, and we're using either exit tickets or informal interviews of students in the classroom to determine the percentage of kids who are actually mastering the content or making progress toward it. If every student in the class is achieving mastery, the content is likely too easy. If nobody is mastering it, it's potentially too hard.

What we're looking for is *progress* toward mastering the content, which can only exist if the teacher is impeccably clear about what they're teaching and what success looks like. Once the teacher is clear on the steps for success, they need to explicitly model those steps for students (this is detailed in Chapter 6). This means that as a coach or an observer, you shouldn't be wondering what kids are working on when you walk into a room. What they're working on should be incredibly clear from the objective, and how they get there should be impeccably clear from the steps that the teacher has shared and modeled and is currently giving feedback on.

To get these data, interview (whispering) a subset of five to seven students: "What's your objective today? What are you trying to accomplish? Why does it matter? What steps are you taking to get there?" If students can't answer any of these questions, we need to coach the teachers specifically around writing measurable objectives, clarifying steps for success, sharing those objectives and steps with students, and explicitly modeling those steps.

Strand 3: Rigor

This final strand targets what we call deep engagement, or *rigor*. Rigor is that point at which the kids walk out of the classroom a lot more tired than the adults. Students are asking questions. They're working in pairs or teams. They're figuring out the steps on their own. They're looking at a problem on the board, reflecting on it, and then writing down what they believe that day's objective is going to be.

Teachers might be saying something like this: "Please turn to your neighbor and share how you got to school today. Explain whether that's the most efficient way for you to get here. If it is, explain why. If it's not, what might be a more efficient way? Feel free to be as creative as you'd like. Students on the window side of the room will go first. Raise your hand if you're going first. We're going to have two minutes to do this. I'm going to let you know when we're at one minute, and then you're going to switch. First person, you're talking the entire first minute, so make sure you're ready to back up your ideas."

Of course, these directions should likely be on a slide as they're quite dense.

In Strand 3, we're looking for the following behaviors:

- Kids are working in groups in which each student has a clearly defined role (so not one student is doing all the work).
- Students respond to other students versus the teacher always responding to them.
- Students are reflecting and writing down their thinking.
- Teachers are cold-calling.
- Students are using academic language.

Common Pitfalls to Avoid

There are quite a few pitfalls here, so take note.

Collecting Data Without a Plan

Avoid gathering data reactively or without aligning them to school goals, frameworks, and student outcomes. By doing this, you risk wasting large amounts of time and frustrating your staff. It may be true that in Mr. Smith's class, he shows a video clip at the beginning of every class. You may think that's a waste of instructional time. But is that something you all have decided you care about? Are students watching it? Are they writing during it? Is it having a positive impact on student outcomes?

Years ago, a leader was frustrated because a teacher wasn't "excited" enough. She was teaching 2nd graders and had a very dry demeanor (according to the leader). We asked what the students were producing and if they were excelling. We asked if being excited was something that *needed* to happen at that school. Did leaders agree? Did staff know? Of course, these answers were no. To be clear, we'd rather teachers be excited than not, but that's not the point. Create a clear plan so that the data you collect are both relevant and usable.

Using a Top-Down Approach

Designing data systems or tools without consulting teachers and school staff will undoubtedly lead to poor buy-in, low participation, or irrelevant data. Keep teachers and staff well aware of the data you'll be collecting throughout the school—and why you're collecting them.

Using Data for Compliance

Treating data collection activities as a box-checking exercise to meet district or state requirements is a quick way to erode staff and teacher trust. This discourages authentic engagement and school improvement efforts. Frame data as a tool for growth, not as a tool for judgment or punishment.

Having Inconsistent Data Collection Practices

Here, different leadership team members are using different methods or tools to collect data. A failure to use the same methodology will ultimately result in data that are unreliable or data that can't be compared in a meaningful way. It's vitally important to standardize data collection procedures and provide aligned coaching and training to leaders.

Failing to Build Data Literacy

Leaders often assume that their staff members know how to analyze and interpret data. In the absence of training on data literacy and analysis, folks are likely to misinterpret and possibly misuse data. You will need to provide professional development on data literacy and how to analyze data in a meaningful way.

Ignoring the Human Side of Data

Leaders often default to focusing only on numbers and ignore context or qualitative input. Meaning, it might be true that Ms. Nailon's 3rd period class is averaging 58 percent on task, which is quite low. But maybe this is a significant improvement. Maybe she's worked tirelessly to get to this place, and maybe this 58 percent is the highest for that class all day. Only sharing the 58 percent would be a mistake here, and this myopic view misses key insights about school culture, student experience, and staff morale. Ensure that you pair quantitative data with qualitative methods. Do not let teachers off the hook or excuse poor data *because* of these pieces (e.g., "That's the worst class in the school, so good job getting them even partially on task"). No. Fifty-eight percent might come with context, but it's still 58 percent.

A Data Collection Template

You can use the template shown in Figure 8.1 to track on-task student behaviors during classroom observations. The conversation that follows illustrates how the principal will use this template to base a discussion in solid data.

Figure 8.1
Data Collection Template

Time	Number of Students On Task	Teacher Actions	Student Outcomes
11:05	25/27	Circulating with clipboard as students work on the Do Now	25 students are completing work 2 students have heads down
11:10	24/27	Uses one voice signal: "I need all eyes on me, pencils down, and silence in 3, 2, 1."	24 students stop working immediately 2 students continue working 1 student has head down
11:15	22/27	"At this time, all eyes are on me and pencils are down. We are not working on the Do Now anymore."	3 students continue working on the Do Now 2 students have heads down
11:20	20/27	Passing out linking cubes: "Please leave these on your desk, and don't touch."	7 students begin to play with linking cubes

A Conversation About Collecting and Sharing Data

Note that while this conversation *is* essential, it doesn't meet our bar for what an essential conversation is—a conversation about resetting expectations. However, we included it here as a strong example of how data can inform a conversation with staff.

Questions to Keep in Mind

- What does "good" look like?
- Are people clear about that?
- Are people meeting that bar?
- Where are the gaps?
- What do I need to address immediately?

The Context: A principal shares data from a classroom observation to address off-task student behaviors with the teacher.

The Conversation

Principal Davis: Thanks for taking the time to meet! I want to talk through some data from the observation I did yesterday during your Do Now and then transition to the math manipulatives. My goal is to support you in increasing students being on task through tightening transitions between activities. Sound OK?

Mr. Lee: Absolutely. I appreciate the feedback. I've been trying a few different things with attention signals, and I'm still refining how I use them.

Principal Davis: That makes sense. I took structured notes every five minutes. At 11:05, you were circulating with your clipboard, and 25 out of 27 students were on task. That's strong task data. Two students had their heads down—do you know what was going on there?

Mr. Lee: Yes. One of them, Jasmine, didn't sleep well the night before. The other, Terrell, sometimes shuts down when he's unsure how to start. I meant to circle back to him.

(continued)

Principal Davis: Got it. At 11:10, you used a clear one voice signal: "I need all eyes on me, pencils down, and silence in 3, 2, 1." Twenty-four students responded immediately, which is a strong response rate. Two kept working, and one still had their head down. How did that feel in the moment?

Mr. Lee: Honestly, better than usual. I've been working on consistency with the signal, and I noticed more kids responded right away.

Principal Davis: Great! It's clearly having an effect. One thing I noticed at 11:15 is that even after a second prompt, three students kept working on the Do Now, and two still had their heads down. You didn't address them.

Mr. Lee: I typically give them a nonverbal cue or a quiet redirection. But in that moment, I was also trying to set up for the activity, so I might have missed the chance.

Principal Davis: Let's look at 11:20, when you passed out the linking cubes. You said, "Please leave these on your desk, and don't touch." But seven students started playing with them immediately.

Mr. Lee: Yeah, I noticed that, too. I think I should have been more explicit about the expectations. Maybe I should have modeled what "not touching" looks like. I also hadn't assigned materials managers, so it was a bit chaotic.

Principal Davis: That's a great reflection. So what I'm seeing and hearing is this: The voice signal is effective, but setting expectations for materials and then redirections could use a boost. Do you agree?

Mr. Lee: Absolutely. I would just add that I think both they and I would benefit from some praise for the students meeting those expectations before I jump to the redirection.

Principal Davis: I love that idea. Let's script out some directions for using those math manipulatives. I think if we can get this down and practice the directions and praise a dozen times right now, we'll get that on-task behavior up to closer to 100 percent.

Mr. Lee: Thanks. I'm glad we're digging into this with actual data—it really helps pinpoint where to focus.

9

Practice Real-Time Coaching

When Michael was in high school, he had a crush on a girl named Sarah. One night, before a big basketball game against a rival school, Michael and his friends went out for pizza. They wolfed down their slices and strolled into the school gym right before tip-off. Just then, Michael noticed his crush, Sarah, sitting in the stands. She waved for him to come over. She asked him to sit next to her, and for the entire game, they cheered, chatted, and laughed.

After the game, Michael walked into the bathroom before heading out. He was elated. But suddenly he noticed that he had pizza sauce on his face and that it had obviously been there the entire time he was talking to Sarah. When he asked one of his friends why he hadn't told him about the sauce, the friend replied, "I didn't want to embarrass you."

Real-time coaching is a strategy that has sent chills down the spine of many a school leader. They think it's disruptive and even disrespectful to teachers. It is, however, a move that separates exceptional leaders from the rest and that helps build extraordinary schools among the ordinary schools.

Real-Time Coaching

What It Is

Real-time coaching refers to the actions of a coach, school leader, or anybody charged with developing and coaching an educator in the moment, while they're engaging in their job. For the purposes of this chapter, we'll focus on the leader- or coach-teacher relationship. But every leader in your building should be giving feedback in the moment to others. For example: "AP Simmons, please speak to the teachers chatting in that corner. We need them to separate and spread out so they can actively supervise students during this recess block. Can you please do that now?"

Why It Matters

Real-time coaching is a necessary aspect of any highly effective school because it enables leaders to bring about change for teachers and students *in the moment*. Let's say that a leader is observing in a class and the teacher is giving directions. The students aren't understanding, and they start expressing frustration and maybe even act out. What do leaders often do? They redirect the students. But the moment they leave, students are back to misbehaving. The issue here is the teacher's directions, so by redirecting the students, they're missing a valuable opportunity to coach the teacher. You can shift things *right then* by coaching them up, but instead, after you leave, you send an email to the teacher or set up a meeting for a few days later. By then, this same situation may already have happened dozens of times. The result? Teachers get frustrated with kids, students get frustrated with teachers—and everyone gets frustrated with you.

Why? Because *everyone* here is aware that things aren't going well. Whether you realize it or not, they're looking to

(continued)

you, the leader, to change things. When you walk out without interceding in a positive way, you're sending a message that you're either unwilling or unable to do anything about it. Think about how that feels to a teacher who needs support. Think about how that feels to an 11-year-old who's counting on you.

Best Practices for Staff Rollout

You may notice that we're going a little out of order in this chapter. We normally start with "best practices for planning," follow that with "best practices for staff rollout," and end with "best practices for execution." But we're not doing that here. Because real-time coaching can be such a divisive topic, we want to share the rollout language first. We included planning *after* execution, simply because the planning here depends on the coaching meeting that takes place before it.

The rollout for real-time coaching can encompass whole-group messaging, individual messaging, or both. Let's look at a sample dialogue between a coach and a teacher. If you plan to message the whole group, modify the script accordingly.

A Conversation with a Teacher About Real-Time Coaching

Questions to Keep in Mind

- What does "good" look like?
- Are people clear about that?
- Are people meeting that bar?
- Where are the gaps?
- What do I need to address immediately?

Context: The coach is going to inform a teacher that they'll be providing them real-time coaching.

The Conversation

Coach: I'd like to discuss a new support I'll be providing for you: real-time coaching.

Teacher: OK.

Coach: It's part of a schoolwide shift where we're really committing to influencing instruction in the moment. I'll be providing feedback in class when I see something I can support you with, as opposed to sending you an email about it later that day.

Teacher: Yeah, it sounds good, but I'm worried that the students will think I'm doing something wrong if you're stopping me and giving me feedback while I'm teaching. I don't feel comfortable with that.

Coach: I totally hear you. First, this is about support and not about anything punitive. So every time I give you real-time feedback, the goal is just about improving student outcomes—and certainly *not* about getting you in trouble.

Teacher: I get it, but I still don't feel great about it. The kids will still assume the principal thinks I'm messing up.

Coach: That leads me to my second point. I'm going to ensure that my feedback occurs in one of two ways. The first will be *whisper feedback*, in which I step over to you and, without students hearing, share something that I believe will have a better effect on students.

Teacher: OK. That sounds all right.

Coach: And the second is this. When I do interject, I'll raise my hand and ask a question. Something like, "Mr. Wilson, how long do students have to complete this?" That way, it doesn't seem as though you've done anything wrong—which you haven't. Instead, it feels like I'm just looking for clarification.

Teacher: Really?

(continued)

Coach: Yep. It's important that students see you as the expert in the room. I'm going to do everything I can to ensure that, while also making sure I support you and your kids in the moment.

Teacher: Thanks! It might be a little weird, but I'm open to trying it.

Best Practices for Execution

If you start real-time coaching just calling out anything you're seeing in the moment in a classroom, teachers will become frazzled, shudder when you walk into their rooms, and feel stressed beyond belief when you enter (some stress is normal, as you're the leader). We use four distinct strategies for our real-time coaching: signaling, whisper coaching, questioning, and modeling. For these to work, though, there has to be agreement and some practicing in advance.

Signaling

The first, and least invasive strategy, is signaling. Signaling occurs when a coach stands in the back or side of the classroom and, using a previously agreed-on signal, signals to the teacher to do something they're not currently doing. A hand moving back and forth could signal that it's time to start scanning the classroom to determine if students are meeting expectations. A plus sign made with two fingers crossing each other could indicate that it's time to praise someone. A hand in the air could mean that a one-voice signal should occur. A finger writing could be a signal for the teacher to ask all students to write. The teacher should be able to see the coach's signal, although it's preferable that students do not. What's important here is that there's been agreement on the signal and that the coach has practiced this with the teacher beforehand, so the teacher knows exactly how to respond. You do not want a teacher staring at you, confused, as you're signaling in the back of the room.

Whisper Coaching

Whisper coaching is more invasive, but students are still unaware of what's being said. In this strategy, the coach is standing relatively close to the teacher. When the teacher needs to do or say something differently to impact students, the coach steps over and whispers that suggestion in the teacher's ear, and then the teacher follows through with it.

A whisper might sound like, "Let's check for understanding," "Let's praise five students," "We don't have all students' attention; let's reset the expectations," or "Let's ask students to write something down about this, and then we'll cold-call afterward." Some of you may not be comfortable with standing in such close proximity to the teacher. If so, skip this technique, but know that it's available.

Questioning

Questioning can happen from any location in the room. After a teacher does something or says something that you think is unclear, such as concerning the sound level desired in the classroom for a given activity, you, as the coach, can interject with "Excuse me, Mr. Green, can I interject here? Can you reset those expectations for sound? I'm not sure all the students are clear on them." This likely would occur because the students are still making noise, even though the teacher has just requested their silence. The coach intercedes because they want to make sure the *teacher* is empowered to reset those expectations. Or a question might sound like, "Dr. Kelly, can I interject for one moment? Could you remind the kids of the steps they need to take to master today's objective? I just want to make sure everybody's totally clear so we can have as successful a class as possible."

Questioning is great. It's our personal favorite technique. Although it's invasive, it also defers to the teacher. For example, the coach might ask the teacher, "Excuse me a minute, Mr. Coleman. Do you see any students who are currently meeting the expectations?" To which the teacher might nod and respond, "Thank you, Amy, Sharifa, and Tiffany—thank you, all three of you—for silently copying down today's objective."

Modeling

This is where the coach or leader just enacts the practice themself. A teacher might say, "All right, students, when I say 'go,' I'd like everybody to annotate pages 9 and 10; look up when you're done." The coach might add, "And please take four minutes to complete this." Or a teacher might say, "Who can tell me what we worked on yesterday?" The coach might add, "Mr. Sellman, can I interject for a second? Scholars, please jot down two things you remember from yesterday's lesson."

Modeling is the most invasive strategy of the four. It's particularly helpful for teachers who are really struggling and who just need somebody to do it for them as they watch and learn. Really advanced teachers may also welcome such feedback; they're so good that if they miss something, some co-teaching from their principal will not in any way undermine them.

Real-time coaching needs to happen. Imagine a coach of a sports team waiting until after the game to tell their players they need to do a better job at x, y, or z. This is insane. They need to be saying things in the moment. Real-time coaching is what great teams and great players do. It's certainly what you, as a great coach and leader, should do—and it's what your team deserves.

Best Practices for Planning

Before any coaching meeting ends, ensure you do the following.

Clarify Your Strategy

Decide on a real-time coaching strategy, one that's directly connected to the specific action the teacher was just coached around. Too often, coaches start signaling to teachers who, in the moment, have no clue what the signal is supposed to mean.

For example, let's say that you just practiced giving clear directions because the teacher often forgets to add the time limit. To remind the teacher to do this, the coach might point to their watch. If the teacher forgets to ask students to write down their thoughts on a topic before calling on them, the teacher and the leader could agree on questioning as a strategy: "Mr. Trugman, can I interject for a moment? Can we ask all students to write a response to your question before we call on anyone?"

Practice the Strategy

This might seem self-evident. The teacher needs to know what the strategy will sound like and how they should respond—*before* they get into the classroom with actual students. An unfocused, overwhelmed, or distracted teacher might simply ignore a cue they're unfamiliar or uncomfortable with. In your coaching session, practice using the strategy several times so the teacher gets comfortable responding to it accordingly. You don't need to build mastery here, just comfort.

Common Pitfalls to Avoid

Leaders may be reluctant to engage in real-time coaching for a variety of reasons.

Fearing It May Not Work

Let's say a coach pauses a lesson and asks a teacher to get the students' attention because they're not listening to the directions. The teacher tries, and it doesn't entirely work. Then the coach tries, and even if it's better, it's not perfect. That's embarrassing! You're supposed to be able to do this! So school leaders may just avoid it. But let's be honest: As leaders, the potential for being embarrassed should never be an obstacle to student success, even if it feels like dying in the moment. Talk to the teacher about how things improved slightly but how there's still work to do. Then, dust yourself off and get back at it.

Thinking It's Disruptive

The fact is, if a teacher is struggling, and kids are wandering around the room throwing tissues at one another, and they're tapping their pens, humming, and tipping their chairs back, disruption is already the norm there. A school leader coming into this classroom and saying, "Hey, Ms. Green, can we pause for a second and reset the expectations here?" is *not* a disruption. It's actually a welcome act of support. Or maybe the teacher is competent around classroom culture but typically fails to give clear instructions about an activity. Instead of 20 students all asking 20 different questions or asking the same question 20 times, it makes more sense—and will result in *less* disruption—to interrupt Mr. Boyce and provide coaching in that moment.

Now perhaps the teacher is highly skilled. As such, they're well positioned to try new things. If you or the teacher are worried that students will wonder why the principal has come into their classroom to observe, you can frame it this way: "Hey, everyone, over the course of the next 10 weeks, you're going to see me in your class a lot. I asked Mr. Jones's permission because we're working together to ensure you're getting the best education possible. When you see me here, please don't think, 'Is Mr. Jones in trouble?' He's really excited about us trying some new and different strategies, and I'm thankful to him for being so open to this. And I'm thankful to all of you in advance for being open to the coaching I'm providing."

You say that to students, and they're going to be totally fine with it. There will be nothing "disruptive" about it.

An Essential Conversation with a Coach About Real-Time Coaching

Questions to Keep in Mind

- What does "good" look like?
- Are people clear about that?
- Are people meeting that bar?
- Where are the gaps?
- What do I need to address immediately?

The Context: A coach expresses concerns to the leader about "interrupting" in the classroom.

The Essential Conversation

Principal: Ms. Emler, I was walking down the hall just now past this classroom you were just leaving. You're coaching that teacher, but it sounds chaotic in there. What's going on? Are you providing real-time coaching?

Ms. Emler: I just didn't want to interrupt the lesson.

Principal: I'd like to share some feedback in response to that. This lesson is *already* interrupted. In the few seconds we've been out here, I've heard no less than 15 students yelling out things. One student is banging on their desk, and I see six students out of their seats. Let's reframe this "not wanting to interrupt the lesson" as an opportunity to make change for this teacher and the students—right now. You know the strategies, you've practiced with the teacher, so let's go back in there and support him now. You have his back, and I'll have yours. Are you up for that?

Ms. Emler: Sure.

Principal: Great. Let's go!

10

Design and Deliver Meaningful Practice

To prepare for her Eras Tour, Taylor Swift spent months singing her entire three-and-a-half–hour set while running on a treadmill (she actually walked quickly during the slow songs and jogged during the faster ones). The pessimist might think that this kind of thing is easier for Swift to do than it is for us. She's wealthy, she has the resources, and she has the time and the space to practice this way. But the optimist knows that a key reason she's where she is at all is because she's *that* committed to being the best she can be and has been operating this way for years—even back when no one knew her name.

Here's the thing: We can all get better. None of us is a finished product. The greatest people who have ever lived have practiced. We should, too.

Designing and Delivering Meaningful Practice

What It Is

Designing and delivering meaningful practice means moving past simply talking to teachers and leaders about what needs to improve. Instead, you script, model, and role-play—not until the other person gets it right, but until they cannot get it wrong.

Why It Matters

Great teams practice. Period. Great players practice. Period. Students don't have time for you to figure things out on your own. They don't have time for you to tell people what to do and hope they do it. They need expert performance from everyone involved. Expert performance comes from practicing.

Best Practices for Planning

Before you'll be able to practice with your teachers, educational assistants, social workers, and others, you'll need to practice with your team. Create fake scenarios and model what it looks like to have an essential conversation: "Let's say that a teacher is two days late submitting their lesson plans. Let's script out what we'll say to them." And just as you're asking your teachers to, provide steps for success. Clarify what "good" looks like so you can provide feedback on those steps.

Design practice around things you all care about: living the values, creating measurable objectives, deescalating students, and so on. Practice with other leaders in a safe space so you're ready to go when you begin practicing with teachers.

Best Practices for Staff Rollout

Focus on two points when you're rolling this out to your staff.

Provide Your Rationale

Explain why you're doing this. Use data, research, and even anecdotal pieces around exceptional performance. Simone Biles practices; Kelly Clarkson practices. Doctors, pilots, lawyers all practice. Explain that if you're going to be the best school in the state—or you're going to be the best at exemplifying your vision statement—you must do things that other teams aren't willing to do. Practice, practice, practice.

Model What It Looks Like

Show your staff what it looks like by modeling a practice session with another leader. Choose something relatable, like praising a student for excellent work. Provide steps for success. Have the other leader practice authentically. Then ask the teachers who are observing this to pretend you just coached *them* and have them engage in the role-play in pairs.

We've seen it hundreds of times. What might feel awkward initially becomes more comfortable with exposure. After the teachers build some comfort with this, we've found that they begin looking forward to practice because they know it's making them better.

Best Practices for Execution

Taking four steps here can nail it.

Name It

People don't like surprises. Name the practice you'll be working on at the beginning of every skill-building meeting. It could sound something like this for an AP or dean: "Today our practice will revolve around praising teachers in their doorways during transitions and redirecting those who aren't." For a teacher, "I'm excited for us to practice cold calling today so we can engage more scholars."

Provide Clear Steps

Ensure that whatever you intend to build a skill around has a clear set of steps for success. If you're not sure how to address a student who was cursing at another student, practice on your own. It may take a few shots, but you'll soon land on an effective response. It's important to note that you may not land on the *best* response. That doesn't matter nearly as much as providing staff with a replicable and memorable set of steps. To this point, a few months ago, we noticed an inordinate amount of students cursing at a partner district (they call them trusts) in England, so we landed on a response. "That language doesn't appropriately represent our value of respect. Please refrain from speaking that way going forward."

It wasn't perfect or brilliant. But it was direct, was anchored in values, and included an action step at the end. On our last visit across the pond, everyone was using this language, and students were responding.

Go for Automaticity

Don't stop repeating the practice when the people you're working with begin to get it right. Keep going until they nail it *every time*. It needs to become an automatic habit or they won't do it. And everyone will be frustrated that nothing has changed.

Provide Feedback Throughout

Your feedback should directly align to the steps you presented. Provide plenty of feedback while the other people are practicing.

Common Pitfalls to Avoid

Don't let well-intentioned coaching run amok. Look for these pitfalls.

Making Learning Feel More Like Shaming

One of the greatest pitfalls of asking anyone to get up and practice a move is the potential for damaging their confidence. If it feels like a public correction or putting a spotlight on something they've done wrong instead of an opportunity to grow, it can easily feel like shaming. Never ask someone to stand up in front of their peers to model some practice without providing a clear context and ensuring that they have had both adequate preparation with the move and adequate time for practice. Embarrassment and defensiveness will undermine the trust and openness that are essential for professional growth.

Failing to Ensure Psychological Safety

For anyone to be vulnerable enough to rehearse or role-play in front of someone else, they need to feel supported, not scrutinized. If the leader initiates a practice moment without attending to the emotional climate or without reading the teacher's cues—they may not be feeling good at that moment about getting up and doing it—the person may interpret the interaction as performative or punitive. Over time, this erodes trust and may lead others to disengage from the coaching process altogether. Creating psychological safety means fostering an environment where risks are safe to take and where efforts to grow are met with encouragement and care. Be careful here, as education is hard. Often, educators have red eyes and marker on their hands and sweaty armpits and looks on their faces like the world is ending. Those are *not* reasons to avoid practice. But do check in first. Don't ask, "Is it OK if we practice?" as you'll often get a no. Instead say, "We're going to practice. Before we do, tell me one thing that went well today and one thing that's top of mind." If the sky is actually falling, you'll find out here and you can pivot. But please pivot rarely.

Skipping the Model

When a school leader directs, let's say, a teacher to "stand up and try it" in a meeting without having modeled first, the teacher is left to play guessing games as to what good looks like. The leader will also then have trouble giving meaningful feedback as they won't know, with impeccable clarity, what good looks like.

Failing to Provide Context

Be sure to explain why you're engaging in a given practice in the first place. If you jump straight into the rehearsal without clearly connecting it to a specific purpose or student outcome, the teacher may question the value of the exercise. They might feel as though they're being corrected for correction's sake, rather than supported in growing a skill that matters. Take time to explicitly connect the practice to an observable student need—such as improving on-task behavior during transitions. This helps ground the work in purpose and meaning.

Failing to Debrief

Even when a practice session goes well, failing to debrief afterward can severely limit its impact. If the teacher practices a move and the moment ends with no feedback or reflection, they're left guessing: *Did I do it right? Should I have done something differently? Was that better than before?* Sure, feedback should happen throughout, but without a debrief, the practice can feel unfinished or hollow. Always follow up practice sessions with "What did you notice? How did that feel?" Ending with specific, affirming feedback can solidify learning and boost confidence.

An Essential Conversation About Designing and Delivering Meaningful Practice

Questions to Keep in Mind

- What does "good" look like?
- Are people clear about that?
- Are people meeting that bar?
- Where are the gaps?
- What do I need to address immediately?

The Context: A teacher is pushing back on the idea of practice altogether, telling you he "has it" and that it's "no big deal." But you know he needs to tighten up his Do Now transitions.

The Essential Conversation

Principal Martin: All right, let's get into some practice.

Mr. Thompson: *(Defensive)* Honestly, I don't really see the point of practicing it now. I know what I'm supposed to say. I do it every day in class.

Principal Martin: I get that. And I want to be really clear. I'm not asking you to perform for me. I'm inviting you to rehearse so we can identify small adjustments that might unlock better results with that last group of students. The data show that you're getting about 75 to 80 percent of students on task immediately, which is good. But the current goal is 90 percent, right?

Mr. Thompson: *(Sighs)* Yeah, I guess so. I just don't want it to feel fake. It's hard to replicate what I'd actually say when there aren't any students in the room.

(continued)

Principal Martin: Totally fair. Think of it like athletes reviewing film or actors running lines. It's not about perfection—it's about refining the delivery. What you say is good. But *how* you say it—your presence, pacing, pausing before you speak—those are the details we can sharpen. It'll take a few minutes, but the results will be long-lasting. Let's try one version of the signal.

Mr. Thompson: *(Still hesitant)* OK. But you're not recording this, right?

Principal Martin: Not at all. Just us. No clipboard, no camera, just support. And by the way, if we do record, let's do it on *your* phone. This way, you can keep it or not. But no one will have it but you.

Principal Martin models here.

Mr. Thompson: *(Stands up)* All right; let's see. *(Delivers in a calm, clear voice)* "Class, I need your full attention. Pencils down. Eyes on me in 3 . . . 2 . . . 1."

Principal Martin: That was solid. Your tone had authority, and you gave just enough pause at the start. Want to try it again? But this time, scan the room first, as though you're trying to make eye contact with a few key students.

Mr. Thompson: *(Slight chuckle)* All right, all right. Let me try that. *(Repeats the signal with more presence)*

Principal Martin: That was it right there! Subtle but strong. That slight pause before you spoke and the eye contact communicated control and calm authority. I really think that version could push your response rate to 100 percent. Let's do a whole bunch more. Are you up for that?

Mr. Thompson: Yeah, that'd be helpful. It's starting to feel like it could make a difference.

Principal Martin: I really appreciate your openness, Mr. Thompson. Practicing in the moment like this isn't always comfortable, but it's the kind of move that sets great teachers apart.

11

Set and Track Coaching Goals

Not long ago, a struggling teacher at one of our partner schools, who was on the verge of quitting, had a staggering breakthrough. Despite feeling like she was drowning in student misbehaviors and perceived disinterest, her assistant principal was able to convince her to stay. The assistant principal didn't achieve this by being "nice" to her or "taking it easy" on her. She didn't achieve it by giving her coffee gift cards or by consoling her during her prep periods. She achieved it through setting, tracking, and referencing data specific to their coaching goals.

At first, they established small, incremental goals about how many students would be on task within one minute of the teacher giving directions for the bell work. Then they increased the percentage of students and decreased the time. Then they set goals around different, more ambitious portions of the lesson.

Slowly, intentionally, the teacher improved. She knew it, too, because each time they hit a goal, they set another more rigorous one. They did this until the teacher was on solid ground. Until she was a person who saw what was possible. A person who knew she could do it.

Coaching Goals

What They Are

Coaching goals are precise goals around both teacher actions (what the teacher is doing) and student outcomes (what the students will do as a result). These goals are set in conjunction with the teacher. They are tracked weekly and during every observation, and the data are shared with the teacher. The share-outs track progress, as well as provide areas of celebration and recalibration.

Why They Matter

If a runner wanted to run a mile in under seven minutes, they would have goals about their time in the first quarter mile, then the second, and so on. They might have goals about how quickly they would need to run the first hundred yards and the last hundred. The initial goals would not enable them to hit their end goal, but as they hit each interim goal, they would set new, more rigorous goals, with always the same goal at the end: running a mile in under seven minutes.

Setting specific goals works in every area of life. The American Society of Training and Development (2014) did a study that was substantiated by Matthews (2015), who found that individuals who committed their goals to an accountability partner were significantly more likely to complete them. The American Society of Training and Development study says that you have a 65 percent chance of completing a goal—*if* you commit to someone. If you have an accountability appointment with that person, you'll increase your chance of success by up to 95 percent.

Goals matter when you're developing others and being developed yourself. Set them. Track them. Celebrate them.

Best Practices for Planning

For goals to truly mean something, you and your staff need to believe that when adult actions change, student outcomes change as a result—even for classes that teachers have labeled as "tough," "low," or "bad." Yes, some classes are more challenging than others. Yes, some students will require more support and differentiation than others. And sure, some factors increase the likelihood of misbehaviors or student disinterest. A class *after* lunch might be harder to settle down than the one right before it. If a teacher is teaching middle school math, and some of the students aren't well prepared because last year's math teacher wasn't very effective, it will be harder to get everyone to mastery.

We get it: These are real challenges. What we're suggesting is that they're *surmountable* challenges. You know that "out of control" 8th grade class in your building? Why does everything run smoothly there when Ms. Wilson is with them? Because Ms. Wilson is more skilled than the other teachers. She has better relationships. She's a stronger instructor.

We're not suggesting that it's easy to get everyone to Ms. Wilson's level. We're simply suggesting that if someone can do it, the argument about the "tough" class becomes mostly moot. And the conversation then shifts to *your* ability to develop your people. But for this to be successful, you *must* adopt the mindset that when adult actions change, student outcomes change as a result.

Ensure the following pieces are in place when working with a teacher.

Establish Accurate Baseline Data

Collect data specific to those areas your school wants to focus on in terms of successful teaching. Our Teacher Coaching Framework (https://skyrocketed.org/frameworks) is a great place to start. For example, let's say you want to target getting students more quickly on task. You need to collect data specific to what the teacher is doing and what the students are doing as a result. Using whatever tool you've agreed on, you observe the class and then establish your baseline data: 50 percent of students are currently beginning a task within 30 seconds of the teacher giving directions.

Use Your Framework or Rubric

Now you need to select specific teacher actions to set goals around. You need to know what "good" looks like. "Increasing pacing" is not specific; "giving all directions in 10 seconds or less" is. "Referencing the objective" isn't specific; "referencing the objective three times: at the beginning of direct instruction, at the beginning of guided practice, and at the beginning of independent practice" is.

Set specific teacher action goals (TAGs) that will directly shift student outcomes.

For example, let's say that a teacher gives directions to the class and then typically begins looking at something on their laptop. As a result, students don't start working right away. The teacher doesn't scan the room and praise students who have started to work. They don't redirect those who haven't started, either. So a strong TAG for the following week would be "The teacher will scan the room for the first 15 seconds after giving directions." If the teacher can do this with relative ease, you could add on to the goal: "The teacher will scan the room for the first 15 seconds after giving directions *and* praise a minimum of three students who have met the expectations." As noted earlier, you'll need to model how to praise students, so have the teacher practice this beforehand.

Once you designate the TAG, which you should create in advance and present to the teacher for feedback, it's time for the weekly student outcome goal (SOG). The SOG will use baseline data and will be measured in direct relation to the TAG. If 50 percent of students are currently beginning a task within 30 seconds of the teacher giving directions—that's your baseline data—you must make an educated guess as to how many students will begin working within 30 seconds *if* the teacher is scanning and praising. You might say, "Sixty percent of students will begin working within 30 seconds of the teacher giving directions." You might up that to 70 percent to make it more challenging. Or you might change the time frame because 30 seconds is a pretty long time to hang out before starting: "Sixty percent of students will begin working within 10 seconds of the teacher giving directions." To minimize your time commitment, you might also add "during the bell work portion of the lesson." The idea here is that if you can build this habit in one area, you'll be able to build it in other areas. This also allows for your observations to be more focused because you'll only be looking at specific portions of the lessons.

Best Practices for Staff Rollout

The rollout for this will be less dramatic than those for some of the previous pieces you will have rolled out. If you're coaching teachers, it makes sense that you'll be setting and tracking goals around your work together, so feel free to mention this to the whole group as you roll out coaching. The message may not feel all that memorable to a whole group, however, because teachers will want to know what *their* goals are once you're coaching them. They'll be far more interested in hearing about the rollout once you've paired them up with leaders.

Your team will need serious training to execute this effectively. Use sample coaching data. Visit classrooms together and set fake TAGs and SOGs. Shadow the team as they observe teachers. Overall, the rollout should be easy. It's the execution that can be challenging.

Best Practices for Execution

Let's look at two best practices in executing coaching goals.

Set Clear Goals

This seems obvious, but we're so conditioned as a field to walking out of a meeting, thanking the host—and failing to clarify concrete next steps. Use data from a recent observation (or handful of observations) to set specific goals for both the teacher and their students in every single coaching meeting you have with them. Use the previous goals for launching points. If the last goal was "70 percent will do *X*," the next goal should be "75 percent will do *X*."

Track the Goals

Again, this is obvious, but so many leaders who actually do set goals don't track them. They're going into the teacher's classroom, they're being supportive, and sometimes they're collecting general data—but they're *not* collecting data specific to the goals they set. There are two ways to ensure that goals feel absolutely meaningless: The first way is to set them wildly high and unreachable, and the second way is not to track them. So set the goals. Then track the goals.

Common Pitfalls to Avoid

Here are a few pitfalls to look out for.

A Failure to Track + a Failure to Improve = a Failure to Invest

Getting into better shape puts way less pressure on a person than committing to losing 20 pounds. It's also far more nebulous. But losing 20 pounds? It either happens or it doesn't. And if it doesn't, that person can reflect on the reasons why, develop a new plan, and recommit. If they have a coach as awesome as you, they'd be even further ahead.

The same applies to a teacher being coached. In the absence of tracking—and in the absence of clear progress based on that tracking—disinvestment will arise. The only way to ensure that progress occurs, that the teaching truly is "getting into better shape," is to coach the teacher to continue to build their skill. Talking to teachers about improvement—or worse, not saying anything at all but simply crossing your fingers and hoping for the best—is ineffective. That doesn't lead to change. Practice with teachers, build their skill, provide real-time coaching so they improve in the moment, and share their progress in meetings to drive investment.

Downplaying the Data

Frustrated teachers might get tired of data dominating your conversations. They may even lash out, saying, "My students are more than just data points!" Of course they are. But it's foolish to pretend as though data don't matter in schools. Sure, anecdotal pieces might tell a story that improvement is happening. Fewer students may lash out at the teachers. More students may greet teachers at the door. More students may be doing their work. Or so it may seem. But without solid data, you won't know exactly if improvement is happening—and how much of it is happening—where it really counts. As a leader in Philadelphia often says, "Everyone wants to see little bars turn into big bars." Having the hard and fast data is the only way you will truly drive change.

An Essential Conversation About Setting and Tracking Coaching Goals

Questions to Keep in Mind

- What does "good" look like?
- Are people clear about that?
- Are people meeting that bar?
- Where are the gaps?
- What do I need to address immediately?

The Context: You've overheard the assistant principal tell one of the teachers she's coaching that things are going better in that teacher's classroom—even though the data say otherwise.

The Essential Conversation

"Ms. Lincoln. Can I share something with you? I heard you telling Mr. Gillespie that his class is improving, but the fact is, he's hitting neither his teacher action goals nor his student outcome goals. I've seen no evidence that his class is getting better. I know you're both working incredibly hard in there, but when you tell him, or you tell any teacher, that things are getting better when it's not actually true—when they're not hitting their goals—you undermine your ability to use data going forward. Because, essentially, you're acknowledging that the data aren't accurate. I worry about him getting false hope. Or, worse, feeling defeated, because if this is what 'better' looks like, he may not be noticing anything better about it. Going forward, can I count on you to stick to the data and to use those to encourage him and to provide areas of growth? Thanks so much for hearing me. Is there anything I can do for you?"

PART III

School Culture

12

Ensure Universal Accountability

Years ago, on one of our very first visits to a partner school in Detroit, we were asked to wait in the hallway for the principal who was on her way back from a classroom visit. The hallway was relatively quiet until the bell rang for transition, when hundreds of students spilled out of class.

A girl who couldn't have been more than 13 years old was hunched over, wriggling her way through the pushing and laughing students, all while hysterically crying at the same time. We watched as adult after adult walked right past her. One teacher who witnessed this, the gym teacher, looked at us and said sarcastically, "Welcome to our middle school." When the principal arrived, she, too, noticed the crying student. She addressed the young girl and gave her the support she needed.

Whether it's ignoring a student who's clearly in distress, breezing by a classroom that seems to be in an uproar, or walking past trash that someone has thrown on the floor—by not saying a thing, so many school teams are missing opportunities to reinforce the schoolwide expectations. They're leaving almost everything to the principal, which is inefficient, ineffective, and unfair.

Universal Accountability

What It Is

Universal accountability is the collective responsibility of all staff members to maintain and reinforce the school's standards, priorities, and principles. It's a unified commitment from teachers, support staff, and administrators alike to actively contribute to creating a consistent and supportive environment. Rather than relying on a single person to monitor and correct behavior or practices schoolwide, every adult is empowered to speak up, take the initiative, and ensure that the school's mission is reflected in daily actions and decisions.

Why It Matters

Universal accountability means it's everybody's job in the building to uphold the expectations. *Everyone* is responsible for making sure that what you say you care about is being upheld schoolwide.

Accountability: It's Not a One-Person Job

Too often, accountability is left exclusively to the leader (or multiple leaders). Sometimes the leader has caused this situation because they haven't empowered staff members to hold everybody accountable to the expectations. That's when people walk past a crying student and don't do a thing. *That's not my job,* they think. *That's not my responsibility. It's up to somebody else.* Or even, *I want to help that student, but will people think it's weird if I say something? I don't want to make anyone angry.*

Of course, you don't want a school where everybody has their nose in everybody else's business. We're not suggesting that your staff of 50—leaders, teachers, operations staff, and educational assistants—just run around telling people how to do their jobs. But yes, everyone should pick up trash if they see it. Everyone who sees an upset student in the hallway should approach them and ask if they need anything or, at the very least, notify the person whose bucket that lands in.

Let's say the administrative assistant at the front desk notices lots of students in the hallway playing around during class time when they should be in classrooms learning. They *should* feel empowered to get those students back in their classrooms. If they don't, they certainly should feel empowered to go to the principal, assistant principal, or dean and say, "Hey, here's the thing I just noticed. I wanted to put it on your radar." And they should be rewarded for that with "Thank you" and "Hey, you're really upholding our value of collaboration and teamwork. You're really supporting the culture in this building."

You don't want people to see their work in your building as only specific to what they do.

"I teach 2nd grade. That's my focus. If I hear kids yelling in the hallway outside my classroom, that's none of my business." Oh, in fact, it *is* your business; it *is* your responsibility. At least, it should be.

For some of you, this may feel like a contradiction to the idea we presented in Chapter 4: having really clear roles and responsibilities. Let us make the distinction.

If it's someone's job to plan back-to-school night, someone else shouldn't just start doing it on their own. That's insane, and it's a culture killer. However, if at back-to-school night, there are family members who seem lost or confused about the schedule, that second person (or whoever sees this) should absolutely step over and provide support.

That's how you run a school where everybody is accountable to everybody else. That's how you can have a school that exemplifies universal accountability.

Best Practices for Planning

The following best practices are crucial to create a culture where all staff, regardless of their title, can hold themselves and one another accountable to the shared commitments, expectations, and norms of the community.

Clearly Define Universal Accountability

The best leaders message relentlessly to their teams that everyone is responsible to everyone else and that universal accountability is a thing we practice here. Together, these teams should create scenarios that illustrate that shared understanding to make it concrete. For instance, if a school has a no gum policy, but one teacher doesn't really think it's a big deal if students chew gum, that person is breaking down universal accountability by not following the norms and potentially making every other staff member's job harder as they'll need to redirect those kids. They may hear things that sound like "Mr. Martin lets us chew gum. Why do you care?"

Finally, the leader should be ultra-clear about how universal accountability supports the organization's vision, the health of the team, and student outcomes.

Align Accountability to Values

There should be a straight line between what you have established as universal accountability as a practice and the school's vision, values, and goals. As an example, let's go back to our Lucas High School vision: *At Lucas High School, we provide a transformational educational experience to students of all abilities and backgrounds. We never waiver from empowering our students, families, and staff to achieve all that they are capable of, while providing A+ support and guidance every step of the way.* Let's say a teacher hears another teacher refer to some students with learning differences as "low" or "slow" and maybe even "annoying" because of those things. They can choose to ignore those things. Or they can remind that teacher that Lucas High is here for students of all abilities and backgrounds, not just the ones who are easy to teach and do whatever you say.

Universal accountability practices cannot just be a policy or saying; they have to be deeply embedded in what and how you believe adults should act.

Develop Tools and Training

Leaders will need to carefully craft and plan how they will develop and prepare their teams to uphold such a culture shift. The best leaders use role-play scenarios, present case studies, and provide clear protocols on how to give feedback. Your team will need to be developed on how to give such feedback and how to hold others accountable, as well as how to receive feedback without being defensive.

Best Practices for Staff Rollout

Like any new initiative, universal accountability and its associated practices must be rolled out thoughtfully.

Start Small

Create a safe environment by getting your staff into small groups or pairs. Using the scenarios you've created, have folks practice giving feedback to each other about things that don't meet the bar at your school. Then move to bigger, more heterogenous groups: veterans, newbies, primary, high school, ELA, and math all together. Continue practicing.

Provide Ongoing Professional Development

Be sure to continually review this training. Recognize successes and address areas of growth in group meetings, as well as in meetings that target staff performance.

Best Practices for Execution

These best practices will help ensure success.

Be Quick and in the Moment

Conversations on universal accountability should be low stakes, be short—less than 30 seconds long—and focus on that one missed opportunity, as opposed to a more general discussion on the topic.

Affirm and Redirect Often

Affirm folks by pointing out and praising them for positive behavior that reflects what's been decided as important. When redirecting adults, be mindful of your tone, approach, and rationale. When your team sees that their behavior has an effect on the overall success of the organization—and that you recognize and prioritize it—it will become just as important to them.

Lead the Way

Consistently hold all members of the community to the high expectations you set for the staff. Avoid showing preferential treatment. And even if it's not always appropriate to redirect staff in the moment, let's say if you're running PD for 100 people and 5 people walk in late, talking, and with iced coffees in their hands (so you know they grabbed coffee before the meeting), and you don't want to stop and have that conversation right then, know that everyone saw it. If it never happens again, they'll know you said something. If it happens next week, they'll know you balked.

Considerations for Special Education

It's important that while you're coaching everyone on your staff to see everything that happens in the building as their responsibility, they don't see that as everything *except* special education.

Michael will often share stories of well-meaning friends and neighbors who simply don't engage with his autistic son. Not because they don't like him or because they're uncaring but because they don't know what to say. They lack the language. And because they won't know what to do if he doesn't respond (which is likely).

Universal accountability goes for everyone. So if a general education teacher sees a student from the special ed program roaming the halls between classes and there's no special education teacher around, they must say something to support that student. At the very least, they should make a call and not think, "That student is special ed. Someone from that department should be along momentarily."

Much like we discussed in Chapter 3, define universal accountability to explicitly include responsibility for students with disabilities, making clear that every adult (general educators, special educators, leaders, and support staff) is accountable for student success, not just compliance or referral completion (McLeskey et al., 2014).

Consider how you will establish clear expectations for adult behavior related to IEP implementation. These behaviors range from how inclusive instruction is defined to how asset-based language is used. Unclear or uneven adult behaviors and actions lead to inconsistent support for students with disabilities (McLaughlin & Rhim, 2007).

Use the concepts in this chapter to address misalignment immediately and directly, anchoring feedback in the school's vision and adult expectations when practices, language, or decisions undermine equitable access or instructional quality for students with disabilities (Fixsen et al., 2005).

Embed accountability measures into your daily systems. Do not create something new with additional steps. Include your special education priorities in walkthroughs, coaching cycles, meeting agendas, and data reviews, so follow-through for students with disabilities is routine rather than reactive (Billingsley et al., 2020).

Common Pitfalls to Avoid

There are two pitfalls to look out for here.

Inconsistent Modeling by Leaders

Failing to uphold universal accountability continually and across the board with all members of the staff will surely undermine the organization's culture. This is the fastest and most effective way to erode trust and influence within your organization. That includes *you* and your leadership team. You must be open to both holding people accountable and *being* held accountable. You must not resist authentic feedback.

Fear of Conflict

Don't avoid accountability simply to maintain harmony. In fact, *not* holding folks accountable disrupts organizations in greater ways than when folks don't meet expectations and are spoken to about it. Dissolve any conflict by basing your affirmation or redirection in vision, school values, adult expectations, or goals. This will allow you to create a culture where universal accountability and accountable conversations are discussed, implemented often, and the norm.

An Essential Conversation About Ensuring Universal Accountability

Questions to Keep in Mind

- What does "good" look like?
- Are people clear about that?
- Are people meeting that bar?
- Where are the gaps?
- What do I need to address immediately?

The Context: The principal ties actions to values (affirmation) and highlights the importance of schoolwide accountability (redirection).

The Essential Conversation

Affirmation: Instead of saying, "Ms. Smith, thank you for being at your doorway," tie your comment to your values by saying, "Ms. Smith, you're modeling our value of 'students above all' by being in your doorway. Thank you for that!"

Redirection: Instead of saying, "Mr. Murphy, the expectation is that all teachers are standing at their door during every transition," tie the expectation to something that is universal and important. You could say, "Mr. Murphy, please step into your doorway. Remember, we're going all in on student belonging this year. A smile or handshake from you will make a difference."

13

Create and Communicate Your Culture Systems

Sometimes, when we're in schools, we'll ask the principal and members of the culture team, "What's supposed to happen in a classroom if a student balls up a piece of paper and whizzes it at the teacher's head?" Some will say it's a call to the dean; some will say the student will lose a point on their token economy system; some will say the teacher will send the student to the office.

"OK," we continue, "so let's say the dean is called and removes that student. What happens next?" We ask similar questions about teachers writing referrals, about entering those referrals into the system, about parent communications, and about follow-up with teachers after student misbehaviors.

The answers are almost *never* aligned. These school leaders are, in *most* cases, making these answers up on the spot.

For example, we were recently working with a school team where one of the deans was saying that he didn't think one infraction was enough to warrant suspension for fighting. He thought three fights should get you suspended. The rest of the leadership team vehemently disagreed. They asked our opinion. We agreed with the people who thought that one time warranted a suspension.

But that's not what's most relevant here. What's important is that this team hadn't clarified this system, which leads to unnecessary confusion—and, quite frankly, to a huge waste of time for leaders who should have already figured this out.

Sure, context matters. Two students who've *never* been in trouble, who are playfully pushing in the lunchroom, would warrant a different consequence than a student just back from suspension who punches a classmate in the teeth just because. But if a student who has never, ever been in trouble punches a classmate in the teeth just because, they should receive the same consequence as the students who misbehave often. Otherwise, every call has the potential to be a free-for-all.

Some schools have airtight culture systems that make a lot of sense. But in these places, many people aren't following them. Most schools don't have systems that make a lot of sense. They're outdated, incomplete, and often hard to find. As you can imagine, people aren't following them. And some schools don't have any systems at all, so adults must make things up in the moment. When that happens, students are unsure of the expectations, and teachers and families are frustrated by the inconsistencies and lack of follow-up.

Culture Systems

What They Are

A culture system is an intentional set of structures, expectations, and routines that govern how the team works in shaping the overall environment of the school. It's the way your school community operates day to day to create safety, a sense of belonging, and joy. These actions are balanced with accountability and equity for both students and staff.

Why They Matter

Every school needs to have a well-designed, predictable, and easy-to-follow culture system that everyone in the building not only is aware of but actually adheres to. This includes how you celebrate students, your response to student misbehaviors, how quickly you turn around referrals, what happens when a student brings an illicit substance to school, your communication with teachers and families about those things, and how quickly you update your systems to ensure everybody is in the loop about what's happening with a student in need. Following these systems ensures predictability, consistency, and ease.

Best Practices for Planning

To ensure success, keep the following in mind.

Create Your Culture Vision and Goals

As a leadership team, you will need to create an extension of your schoolwide vision and goals to include a clearly defined culture vision for leaders, teachers, and students. A set of actionable goals that can be tracked and measured using a shared and accessible platform should accompany this vision.

Build the Foundation

A great start for a highly functional culture system is to ensure you have a universal accountability model in place. Sure, deans of students will likely run lead on assemblies, student celebrations, student discipline, reinstatement hearings, and expulsions. But everyone should feel accountable for ensuring that the culture of the building is safe, predictable, and setting students up for success. Here is a nonexample: A teacher gets frustrated with a student who is talking during instruction. Instead of following the classroom ladder of redirection and maybe consequences, and instead of calling a dean, they simply send the student out into the hall. "Go find Mr. Glenn!" Now that student is walking the halls, without a pass, looking for an adult who may be three floors away. So yes, it's the culture team's responsibility to run lead here, but it's everyone's responsibility to ensure the system is executed with consistency.

It's a mistake to see school culture as *only* discipline. Yes, it's often heavily about discipline, but part of this system should include creating a yearlong culture calendar with clear timelines for events, which include special recognition dates, spirit weeks, and incentives.

Establish a Ladder of Celebrations and Consequences

As a school community, you need a consistent and scaffolded ladder of celebrations and consequences that staff and students understand. Schools should decide on positive behaviors to reinforce for students and behaviors students should be dissuaded from exhibiting. To keep this doc manageable, we suggest having overarching topics and then listing subtopics below them. For instance, on the positive side, you might list teamwork as a behavior to celebrate. Below that you might write, "being kind to new students, helping a student pick up their books, grabbing the missing work for a student who is absent," and so on. Staff will likely need to make some judgment calls when a student exhibits teamwork around something not listed. The same goes for an overarching topic like minor disruptions. Underneath that could be pencil tapping, getting out of seats without permission, talking during silent work time, and so on.

Moreover, it's important to have a written document that all staff members are familiar with that clearly outlines how the school will affirm students for doing the right thing and how they will redirect students and hold them accountable when they don't meet expectations.

Be sure your cultural systems are balanced. Basing your system in restorative practices and in a positive behavior incentive system—and including the voice of students and staff—will help maintain a positive culture.

Best Practices for Staff Rollout

Here are two best practices to consider.

Develop and Calibrate

You will need to spend a significant amount of time training and developing staff on schoolwide expectations. Outline expectations for all major activities in the building, such as transitions, various classroom protocols, lunch, and assemblies. You won't achieve this in a one-shot professional development session. This effort must be ongoing. To make learning concrete and consistent, modeling, culture walkthroughs, and role-playing can help.

Communicate Clearly

Rolling out updates requires clear and consistent communication. Expectations about how students are expected to behave in your school community require overcommunication through multiple formats including family handbooks, newsletters, websites, and daily "culture blasts." Once your culture systems are up and running, ensure timely and solutions-oriented communication with families and students after any incidents. Also, be sure to communicate the positives as well. When students exceed expectations or show deliberate growth, it's on your team to shine a spotlight on these moments.

Best Practices for Execution

Be sure to take the following into account.

Be Present—and Monitor

To ensure adherence to the culture systems you've created, leaders need to be visible at all high-traffic times and in all high-risk areas (bathrooms, halls, at arrival and dismissal). Use frequent walkthroughs and incident data to proactively plan for both celebrations and student support.

Celebrate and Reinforce

Leaders will need to take the time to recognize both staff and students' positive behavior and growth. Implement meaningful rituals and traditions that consistently reaffirm student identity and the school's values.

Considerations for Special Education

Tightly coordinate academics, student support services, and the culture systems to ensure all facets of the school are working in concert. You'll want to know if the student who's been in your office four times this week is also struggling in math. Is he *only* there during math? Does he have an IEP or 504 plan you should know about? Hold regular data reviews and planning meetings that include the culture team, special education leaders, and the school leadership team.

Although you cannot lower the bar for students with special needs, you must make accommodations for them. Simply hoping that they will just "get it" one day is not a formula for success.

Common Pitfalls to Avoid

Avoiding the following will help ensure success.

Inconsistent Implementation

Uneven implementation only serves to undermine credibility. Work to eliminate as much misalignment as possible between classrooms. Work to eradicate inconsistent follow-through on consequences by consistently monitoring implementation. You'll likely never be able to get this perfect. That's not us lowering the bar; it's a reality. But strive to be as aligned as possible. Even 80 percent alignment puts you ahead of nearly every school out there.

Failing to Prioritize Relationships

A heavy-handed and one-sided approach will quickly erode trust and stifle student agency. Be mindful to prioritize relationship building over control.

Poor Communication

Poor communication will kill all your efforts, and your culture systems will come to a screeching halt. Be sure to update families or internal teams to avoid confusion and misalignment within the organization.

Omitting Joy and Fun

Systems that ignore student voice, fun, and joy will fail. Although there's a tendency to focus on the behaviors that are hindering learning and negatively affecting culture, don't forget to, as the old expression goes, catch students doing the right thing. Set up student councils, ask students to take part in assemblies, assign them jobs in the school to empower them, and overall, celebrate their brilliance. For some students, you and your team are the only ones who will.

An Essential Conversation About Creating and Communicating Culture Systems

Questions to Keep in Mind

- What does "good" look like?
- Are people clear about that?
- Are people meeting that bar?
- Where are the gaps?
- What do I need to address immediately?

The Context: A teacher is calling families every night but only to share what students are doing wrong. They aren't making any positive calls.

The Essential Conversation

"Good afternoon, Mr. Craig. Can I share some feedback your way? I was reviewing our call logs, and I noticed that while you're making your required eight family calls per week, they're all about students not meeting expectations. In fact, it looks like you called home for Magnus, Jaden, and Kemberly each of the past three weeks. While I'm appreciative that you're meeting this expectation, I really want to encourage you to do two things: the first is to call the families of students who are having a lot of success in your class. The second is, while there are some students struggling, I'm going to ask that you share *some* wins with those

(continued)

families. I am not asking you to bend the truth or to act as if their behaviors aren't concerning. They are. And I know Dean Watts is working with you on supporting them. But peppering in some wins, even just small ones, might provide a glimmer of hope for families who might feel like things are hopeless. Remember, we go all in for all students. This is a great way for you to continue to do that. Does that work for you? Can I count on you to do this? Thanks so much for hearing me. Is there anything I can do for you?"

14

Define and Embody Culture Team Expectations

Recently, at a Skyrocket retreat, we were discussing the struggles of culture teams around the United States. When we say "culture teams," we're referring to the person or persons in your school who respond to culture issues. This might be someone who ensures that people follow a specific protocol, such as when and how to call parents when there's a concern about student behavior. You might have a designated culture team, or you might just have a dean, an assistant principal, or a teacher leader with two release periods a day who fulfills this function—essentially, the people who'll be executing the culture systems you just read about.

So we asked this question: "During summer training, when teachers and TAs are building skills around instruction, classroom routines, curriculum, and so on, where are the deans?"

After a moment, a team member answered, "Nowhere."

That person was right. Culture team members are typically forgotten when it comes to concrete expectation setting and skill building. They're often left alone to roam the hallways, looking for things that seem "off." Sometimes they're receiving the same training teachers are. Sometimes they even run these trainings. But when it comes to how we make our culture teams better, this is an often missing component of our schools.

Creating the culture system and then executing on what you've stipulated matters. It also matters for those responsible for that creation and execution to have clear expectations for how they're supposed to do that work.

Culture Team Expectations

What They Are

These are clear, detailed, and thoughtful expectations for what culture team members are responsible for; where they should be and how often they should be there; how they should relate to students, staff, and families; and what their turnaround times should be for responding to all things "culture." If you feel you've already fully covered designing this after reading about adult expectations in Chapter 3, we still encourage you to read on. From our experience, even when we feel we've covered everything for the culture team, there's so much else.

Why They Matter

Culture team members are often the least trained and least supported people in school, perhaps because culture isn't the most fun thing to deal with. It's messy and uncomfortable. Leaders usually choose people to do this work who they believe will have good relationships with kids and who will be able to figure the rest of it out themselves.

Recently, when Michael was in a school, one of the deans was outside the office he was in, screaming at a student. When Michael asked the chief academic officer he was meeting with if it was OK for any adults, but in this case, deans, to scream at students, she simply shrugged her shoulders and said, "I don't know." The fact is, most culture team members are not told what to do. So they look it up or they make it up. But the onus is not on them to find out—it's on you, as the leader, to ensure there are rock-hard expectations for culture team members.

Best Practices for Planning

Planning starts with a focus on the following actions.

Clarify the Purpose and Vision

Whoever is responsible for school culture must be clear on its "why" and clear on its "how"—*why* to address school climate concerns and *how* to do that in a way that lifts students up versus disinvesting in them. *Why* inequities should be analyzed and how to eradicate them. *Why* building a more joyful learning environment matters and how to do so.

Establish Clear Roles and Norms

All members of the community should be on the same page here. Parents and students should understand the role of the culture dean or the assistant principal when it comes to addressing infractions, issuing rewards, or administering consequences.

Use Data to Inform Priorities

Instead of acting on assumptions, rely solely on trends from surveys, referral data, incident reports, and attendance logs to drive your day-to-day work and initiatives for change. If your data show a spike in hallway disruptions during the third period transition or an overrepresentation of Black boys in referrals, the team will need to investigate causes and target interventions.

Best Practices for Execution

Ensure successful implementation by following through on these to-do items.

Monitor Data Regularly

Create a cadence of data reporting to ensure there's growth toward goals. This includes both quantitative and qualitative data tracking and monitoring. The best leaders track what's important and what's working, and they find ways to quickly adjust. Regularly conduct "culture walks" to observe and collect data on school climate and tone. Beyond the hard and fast data you'll collect, ask yourself, "Who is the teacher calling on most? Does every scholar have a place of belonging in here? Does one gender get preferential treatment? One race? One religion?"

Prioritize Professional Development

Provide recurring professional development for the culture team. They will need to stay ahead of the curve on restorative practices, de-escalation, and cultural responsiveness, as well as on positive behavioral intervention and supports (PBIS) and similar initiatives.

Stay Adaptive

School culture and climate can shift instantly. External or internal events can quickly influence the environment either positively or negatively. We've seen this recently after elections, during the pandemic, and after instances of racial injustice. Culture team leaders must ensure they have robust systems and procedures in place that are documented in writing to address these things. If they don't, they must be proactive in understanding what the current environment inside and outside the building is. When Michael was a teacher in South Philly, the Philadelphia Phillies won the World Series. The parade route ran right past his school. The culture team decided, with approval from the principal, to give everyone a day off. Not to celebrate, but to avoid dismissing 800 Black and Brown kids into a crowd of 1 million (many drunk) rabid baseball fans. This is the level of responsiveness your team needs.

Considerations for Special Education

In so many schools, staff are used to ignoring students with special needs. Not because they're uncaring jerks, but because they don't want to step on toes, they don't have the language, and they feel like those students are already taken care of.

This is the opposite of what should be happening, particularly with members of the culture team who have an opportunity to ensure their special ed students are being exceptionally well cared for.

Although we won't prescribe a specific amount of touch points for the culture team and students with special needs, they should connect often. And the culture team should know that some students may not respond but that they likely heard and understood everything that was said.

As mentioned above, students with disabilities may receive varying levels of implementation of school culture systems and discipline, for a myriad of reasons. It is important to require and monitor consistent implementation of culture and discipline practices across all adults, reinforcing that accommodations, de-escalation strategies, and positive support are nonnegotiable components of universal accountability (Sugai & Simonsen, 2012). This is best accomplished by focused professional learning and supporting staff to respond to behavior with clarity and consistency, ensuring discipline decisions are predictable, instructional, and aligned to the school's lived values rather than being reactive or exclusionary (Simonsen et al., 2017).

Leadership teams must be data gurus. All discipline data must be disaggregated by disability status to monitor equity, identify patterns of disproportionality, and intervene when systems (not students) are driving negative outcomes (Skiba et al., 2014).

Common Pitfalls to Avoid

You can doom your efforts by failing to take the following into account.

Lack of Clear Vision

The culture team, or whatever that means for your school, cannot expect success without a guiding purpose. An absence of guiding purpose leads to taking on too many projects or losing focus. If a team attempts to overhaul its dress code, lunchroom norms, and social-emotional learning programming all at once, it will struggle to make traction in any area. What matters most? Go all in there.

Inconsistent Implementation

A school's climate should be felt from the moment someone enters your building. When systems and initiatives are not implemented with

100 percent fidelity, they can fall apart and not reach their intended goal. If one grade level or classroom enforces the behavior matrix with fidelity and other classrooms ignore it, this leads to confusion among students and undermines staff credibility.

Basing a System on Rewards

Culture teams will need to foster intrinsic versus extrinsic motivation. This can be developed through ongoing relationship building, leadership opportunities for students, and the language they use. Telling a student who made a bad choice, "That was wrong—don't ever do that again" won't do this nearly as well as saying, "I know you know you messed up. There are consequences for that. But I believe in your ability to come back even stronger from this." It's counterproductive for students to meet expectations *only* because a reward is promised and not because they believe in community respect, the collective vision of the school, and themselves.

Ignoring Staff Culture

A focus on school culture must include a focus on staff morale and cohesion. Often, leaders look only to student behaviors and actions. If you launch a "Be Kind" campaign for students and fail to address the toxic team dynamics among teachers, it's sure to erode trust and positivity. Plus, some of the people you'll need to execute it won't be invested. Ensuring that adult culture is positive remains a foundational principle.

An Essential Conversation About Defining and Embodying Culture Team Expectations

Questions to Keep in Mind

- What does "good" look like?
- Are people clear about that?
- Are people meeting that bar?

- Where are the gaps?
- What do I need to address immediately?

The Context: A school culture team member believes in strong punishments for students who misbehave. She knows the culture manual exists, but she chooses to dole out harsh consequences as she sees fit.

The Essential Conversation

"Hi, Dr. May. Can I have a moment of your time? Great. One of my noticings in shadowing you over the past few days is how much you truly care about our scholars. To see you embrace so many children at arrival, to sit with and chat with so many kids at lunch, and to even play soccer with them, although briefly, during recess was truly special to watch. More important, it makes such a difference for our kiddos. Thank you. One thing I want to flag is the punitive nature of your approach. When Tamara was asked to leave math because of an argument with another student, you gave her in-school suspension for the rest of the day. When Jesse and Latia were playfighting, you suspended them both for two days. While I appreciate your commitment to our culture, none of these punishments is commensurate to their infractions. Furthermore, they're not aligned to our culture system. Going forward, I'm asking that you continue to build those strong relationships with students while also following our system precisely as it was designed. Does that work for you? Thanks."

15

Build Relationships

Years ago, Antonio was coaching a teacher who people in the district said was "a total nightmare" to work with. He heard that she was rude, not open to feedback, dishonest, cranky, and disinterested in being better for kids. A few minutes into their first meeting, Antonio picked up on some of those same vibes. The teacher was talking fast, trying to rush through the meeting, and not looking Antonio in the eye. There was an underlying theme in her language, although she didn't come out and say it directly: She felt like she wasn't being heard. She said things like, "I've told the administration about that," "I've been saying that for years," and "What's the point? It won't change."

Nervous about upsetting a person who everyone had labeled as difficult, he said, "It sounds like you're frustrated because you have a lot to say, and people aren't listening to you." She looked at Antonio for the first time.

"Yeah, I guess that's right," she said.

In that moment, they made a connection. Don't get us wrong. She disagreed with Antonio often, pushed back on feedback she didn't like, and sometimes refused to practice. But according to everyone, she was the best she'd ever been. And Antonio's relationship with her was good. Not great, but *good*. A leader once joked that in our teacher coaching model, there should be a Strand 0 before Strand 1. "Strand 0," they explained, "should be building relationships—because nothing can happen without them." We don't agree that *nothing* can happen without them, but we *do* agree that the best things happen *with* them.

Building Relationships

What It Is

This means intentionally cultivating strong relationships with staff, students, and families through strategic actions, conversations, and connections.

Why It Matters

The work you do is hard. It's often punishing, with challenges feeling a million miles high and wins feeling like they're few and far between. Having strong relationships with people motivates them and you. When there's mutual appreciation, people are willing to do more for one another. And when you're connected, you feel safer going to one another to ask for help.

Best Practices for Planning

People often believe that relationships should form naturally, so the idea of *planning* for this can invite criticism. Attempting to engineer positive relationships can feel like the opposite of authentic. But here's the thing: We *all* attempt to engineer things to make a good impression, get what we want, and get others to like us.

When you went to that job interview for the position you're currently holding, did you wear your pajamas? If you're in a relationship, did you yawn and roll your eyes when you were on that first date?

Michael tells the story of having dinner with the family of his wife, a few months after he started dating her. He took his hat off at the table, a gesture that had no importance for him, but he thought it might be important for his girlfriend's father, a Vietnam veteran who is very big on tradition and formality. So Michael took his hat off—and impressed his future father-in-law.

Similarly, a member of the Skyrocket team used to work at a high-end steakhouse in New York City. One particular server wrote down notes about the people he waited on in a book he could refer to. He noted their names, their professions, their interests, their kids' interests, and where their next vacation was. The next time any of those customers came in, he could say, "Ms. Willis, how was the golf outing in Turks and Caicos?" or "Mr. Reynolds, did Jenny's team win the soccer tournament?" Customers were *blown away.*

Are any of these examples *totally* authentic?

No.

When we're talking about one relationship between two people who've known each other for a while, perhaps things can evolve more organically. But we're talking about something different: the need to connect to hundreds of people—staff members, students, families, community members, in some cases board members, people from the central office, and more. And while it's unlikely you'll build strong relationships with *all* of them, you *can* build strong relationships with many of them, but you're not going to do it by accident.

Start by Making a Commitment

Decide that relationships matter. Decide that connecting with students and staff matters. Decide that families are your partners. Decide that hearing from students, staff, and families is important. (Just to clarify, everyone should be heard, although that doesn't mean that everyone gets their way.) Decide that knowing what people like, who they care about, and what they might be struggling with matters. Your brilliance will only get you so far. Relationships, in our experience, will get you further.

Make a Plan

Schedule town halls to connect with families; schedule phone calls to check in with them. Yes, you'll leave many voicemails and not get a lot of callbacks. Still, those who do call back will be thrilled that you cared enough to call. Schedule time to stop by every classroom every day (depending on the size of your school) to ask if the teacher needs anything. We're not talking about observing or giving feedback. Just, "Mr. Dantley, good morning. Is there anything I can do for you today?"

Learn student names. Learn student names. Learn student names. Dale Carnegie (1981), author of *How to Win Friends and Influence People,* asserted that everyone has the same favorite word: our own name. So learn student names. If someone has mentioned that they're going to rescue a puppy from the shelter over the weekend, jot that down so you can ask them about it Monday.

Best Practices for Staff Rollout

Rolling this out to the whole staff is a bit tricky. There may be pushback about authenticity. For example, if you stop by a teacher's classroom with the genuine desire to promote strong relationships and you ask the teacher if they need something—after you've just rolled out professional development on some relationship-building practice you want the teachers to use—your gesture may well fall flat. Therefore, it's best to keep the official rollout of this push to more intentionally build relationships among the leadership team.

Share research on the importance of workplace relationships. Work with your team to define spaces and places where they can intentionally build relationships: the teacher's lounge, the lunchroom, the playground, during extracurriculars. Ask the team to reflect on how they felt in workplaces where relationships were strong, as opposed to places where they weren't strong. Consider, too, that your team may feel as though *they* fall in that latter category. If that's the case, you'll need to own this and commit to improving those relationships on your own team.

For teachers, stress the importance of building relationships with students and families. Include research on the effect that both positive and negative relationships have on students. Set expectations around parent communications. For instance, ask teachers to make five parent phone calls each week, with more of those phone calls being positive than negative. The phone calls need to be tracked in some kind of shared document. If you have grade-level team leads, they can review these trackers before or during team meetings to ensure those calls are happening.

Best Practices for Execution

These best practices are specific to you and your team.

Note It—and Do It

Just like the friend you keep saying you want to reconnect with—but you never actually do it—this won't happen on its own. A calendar that has this note on Monday, "See all first floor teachers," will remind you to ensure that these connections happen consistently. The reminder is great, but you also have to follow through on what it says. Otherwise, it's moot.

Ask Questions and Listen

You're the boss. Your staff hears from you a lot. Now it's time for you to hear from *them*. "How was your weekend?" "Did you see the Steelers game?" "How did your wife's job interview go?" Avoid the temptation to share a story that mirrors their own: "That reminds me of the time I had a hole in one. . . ." Don't do that. Instead, ask a follow-up question. And remember what they've told you. Asking someone their son's name eight times doesn't make them feel terribly valued.

Be Grateful

Gratitude not only feels great for the receiver but also feels great for the giver. Express gratitude that a staff member is working alongside you. Express gratitude that they're working their hardest for kids. Express gratitude for everything they bring to the team.

Common Pitfalls to Avoid

Watch out for this one.

Being Too Busy for This

Other things will feel more important than this. This focus on building relationships will get pushed aside. You'll miss a week or a month of asking students how their football game went. You'll miss opportunities to ask the facilities person how his 20th anniversary dinner was. You will miss times to connect with those around you. We all do that. But get right back to it. You cannot be too busy to connect with and show appreciation for the people on your team.

An Essential Conversation About Building Relationships

Questions to Keep in Mind

- What does "good" look like?
- Are people clear about that?
- Are people meeting that bar?
- Where are the gaps?
- What do I need to address immediately?

The Context: This conversation is with another leader who says they're too busy to connect with students, staff, and families.

The Essential Conversation

"Ms. Williams, can I share some feedback? I hear what you're saying. We're all very busy. But I'm going to ask you to refocus on what matters most here: the people. Yes, we need to be in compliance and yes, we need to do well on our state assessments. But people perform better when they're appreciated and when they feel connected. We're working together on this, and I'm coaching you to see this not as an add-on that you'll get to when you can, but instead, as a fundamental thing that we simply *do* here. Does that make sense to you? Can you commit to that?"

PART IV

Bringing It All to Life

16

Design and Adhere to Calendars

For so many school leaders, days bleed into days. Friday arrives, and they wonder where the week went. Sometimes this happens for months—and sometimes for entire school years.

You're likely the busiest person in the building. That's because you make everything run. But if you haven't done good planning and don't follow up on things, you'll wind up playing defense most of the time, responding to things as they happen and failing to move the school as far forward as you're truly capable of doing.

One time, while we were meeting with a leader in his office, a teacher knocked on the door. This exchange followed:

Teacher: Do you have a minute?

Leader: Not right now. Is it an emergency, or can we speak later?

Teacher: It's not an emergency. I just wanted to get your opinion on something. What time works?

Leader: Around 2-ish?

Teacher: OK.

Leader: Thanks.

Then the leader wanted to go back to our meeting.

Not so fast. We immediately asked him, "You didn't look at your calendar when suggesting '2-ish,' nor did you write it down anywhere. So, honestly, what's going to happen at 2-ish?"

We appreciated the leader's transparency in responding: "I'm going to forget. She's going to come here, and I won't be here. She'll try to find me in the building and likely won't be able to."

"What then?" we asked.

"Well," he said, "She'll eventually find me at the end of the day. I'll apologize, but I'll feel like an idiot for having made her run around all afternoon looking for me."

"How do you think she'll feel?" we asked.

He thought a moment about this, then replied, "Like I've totally wasted her time, like what she needs doesn't matter to me."

So many leaders operate like this. And it needs to change.

Designing and Adhering to Calendars

What It Is

Leaders should regularly update and adhere to an easy-to-navigate, color-coded calendar that is accessible to other leaders.

Why It Matters

A calendar can be a leader's best friend. And although we didn't coin the expression "failing to plan is planning to fail"—it's often attributed to Ben Franklin—it's relevant here. When a leader intentionally plans a calendar and actually follows it, they will shift from playing defense most of the time to playing offense, while further improving things for adults and kids. Yes, things will always come up. But knowing you have only 20 minutes to respond to something or knowing that you have to delegate the task to someone else because you have an observation coming up and you intend to stick to it—well, that's a level of discipline and freedom that most urban school leaders rarely experience.

Best Practices for Planning

Doing the following will really up your game.

Focus on Planning over Scheduling

Planning involves identifying priorities and using them to drive how you spend your time. Someone should be able to look at your calendar and know exactly what your priorities are. Your calendar should reflect big-picture thinking, what you believe you need to do and why. These are things like classroom observations, coaching, meetings with students and families, and leadership team meetings. This is different from *scheduling,* which is the act of calendaring tasks and meetings to accomplish things you've previously planned (e.g., arrival, dismissal, lunch duty). This also needs to happen. The best leaders find that balance where the big-picture planning is equal to or greater than the tasks that just need to happen every day.

Set Priorities Weekly

At the start of each week (find time Sunday evening or Monday morning), spend time identifying upcoming key goals and deliverables. The times blocked out on your calendar should reflect these priorities. Remove needless recurring meetings or FYIs that you don't even attend or attend to. Use a time management tool to prioritize tasks, such as the Eisenhower Matrix, which sorts tasks into four quadrants based on urgency and importance.

Protect Strategic Time

Reserve blocks for leadership essentials, such as classroom walk-throughs, data reviews, one-on-one meetings, or family engagement. These blocks should be nonnegotiable, not placeholders. If needed, use different colors to differentiate among such priorities as instructional leadership, operations, team development, and external engagement. This is helpful for many leaders who often perceive their calendars to be this sea of blue coming to swallow them up.

Align with School Goals

Your calendar activities should reflect strategic school objectives, both quarterly and annually. Scour your calendar and if a task or meeting is not aligned to those goals, question whether it belongs there. This is important as so many of us have so many things on our calendars that don't matter. Michael jokes that for years, his calendar would tell him to take his vitamins at 1:00 p.m. Instead of taking his vitamins, he just got really good at ignoring his calendar. Once you start ignoring your calendar, you're likely going to be playing defense consistently.

Build in a Margin

School days can be unpredictable. Leave gaps for buffer time between meetings to allow for transitions, debriefs, and unexpected tasks. In addition, block out time on your calendar to address nonpriority items, such as "check and respond to emails," or "flex time," where people can schedule to meet with you or where you can follow up on conversations you were unable to have while you focused on your priorities. If this is funny to you because you're thinking, "Where would I possibly find the time to check my emails?" it's likely because so many of the things we've written about before this aren't happening. You're likely doing too many other people's jobs, responding to issues that would be solved by a clearer culture system, and addressing behaviors that are occurring because of a lack of adult expectations.

Best Practices for Staff Rollout

These best practices will get you started.

Start with a Time Audit

To begin, track how you currently spend your time over the course of one week. Compare that timing with an ideal time allocation—for example, a 60 percent focus on instructional leadership and school culture, a 30 percent focus on more transactional items like being in lunches and at dismissal, and a 10 percent focus on everything else: things like checking emails, returning phone calls, and oh yeah, eating. Use this audit to guide the restructuring of your time.

Share Your Calendar

Don't hide the ball. Leaders should be transparent about how and where they spend their time. Administrative assistants, assistant principals, and coaches should all have some visibility into your leadership team's calendar. Adjust permissions as needed to protect confidentiality.

Establish Calendar Protocols

All staff members need to know the expectations for governing their time. Determine how everyone should handle meeting requests and what the expectations are for recurring appointments. Clarify the rules for prioritization, protected time, and scheduling etiquette. For instance, when two staff members plan to meet, should one send an invite? Should it include date, time, and location? Is it protocol for people to *accept* those invites?

Best Practices for Execution

The following actions can help you get a handle on your calendar.

Review and Adjust Daily

Spend 10 to 15 minutes at the start or end of the day reviewing and adjusting for any changes. If you miss a task or need to miss a meeting, move it immediately to its new spot on your calendar.

Use Alerts and Reminders

We've all forgotten to attend a meeting or arrived late because we were distracted. With everything happening in a school, you can't possibly retain everything that's on your calendar. Set reminders for 10 or 15 minutes before high-priority events.

Include Preparation and Follow-Up Time

Don't just block time for the meeting itself. Be sure to include 10 to 15 minutes (or more depending on what it is) beforehand to adequately prepare yourself for the meeting and the same amount of time afterward to debrief or act on takeaways. Action items and follow-ups will pile up after meetings and can leave you feeling swamped and overburdened—but not if you take the time to immediately act on them or schedule them in your calendar.

Reflect Weekly

On Fridays, ask yourself, "Did I spend time where it mattered? What got in the way? What do I need to adjust next week?"

Considerations for Special Education

The best way to demonstrate that you prioritize special education is by protecting time on calendars for special education priorities. This includes when IEP reviews occur, instructional walkthroughs of inclusive spaces, and collaboration with special educators. How you spend your time as a leader directly influences instructional quality and system coherence (Leithwood et al., 2020). In addition, leaders should constantly monitor the team's calendars as an accountability tool. This is a quick and easy way to regularly audit time spent against stated priorities to ensure leader actions align with commitments to inclusion and high-quality instruction for students with disabilities (Grissom et al., 2015).

This one is tough, but you must find a way to create sacred, recurring, structured collaboration time for general and special educators to plan instruction, review student progress, and align supports, recognizing that inclusive practices improve when collaboration is intentionally built into the school schedule (McLeskey et al., 2014).

Special education should be represented in key leadership meetings and have a dedicated space in all agendas. Include special education in instructional leadership team, culture team, and strategic planning sessions. This strongly signals that serving students with disabilities is central and not peripheral to the school's overall efforts to serve all students (Billingsley et al., 2020).

Common Pitfalls to Avoid

Avoid these common mistakes.

Ignoring Your Calendar

The number one pitfall for leaders lies not in creating a calendar but not using it regularly. This leads to missed opportunities concerning what needs to be done. If you're not using your calendar regularly, you'll struggle to meet your goals and priorities.

Overbooking

Leaders often leave little breathing room in their schedules during the crunch of a school day. This often leads to fatigue and missed opportunities for coaching and supporting your team. Remember, *plan* over *scheduling*.

Falling Prey to Reactive Scheduling

Allowing others, without your oversight, to block out times on your calendar for various activities or meetings that may be important to them can lead to time wasted on low-priority items. Don't let others dictate your workday; provide clear guidance on when and how others should access and use your calendar.

Failing to Schedule Follow-Ups

Schedule follow-ups to meetings on the spot. You or a staff member can send out the invite, but do it in the moment so that it's on the calendar with a reminder. Missing follow-ups often leads to a failure to address action items, as well as confusion and erosion of trust.

An Essential Conversation About Designing and Adhering to Calendars

Questions to Keep in Mind

- What does "good" look like?
- Are people clear about that?
- Are people meeting that bar?
- Where are the gaps?
- What do I need to address immediately?

The Context: Our assistant principal is speaking with their principal, because the principal is missing meetings and deadlines.

The Essential Conversation

"Hey, Mrs. Kaye, can I share some feedback with you? At our last leadership team meeting, you arrived 20 minutes late and shared that you forgot, and for the past two things you were supposed to share with me, the finalized evaluations for Mr. Bremmer and Mr. Gold, you missed both deadlines by days. This pushed my meetings with them back, and I didn't really have a good rationale to share, so I just made it up. You're always preaching that we should be very intentional about our calendars and our time, so I'm a little worried that that's not currently happening with you. On a larger note, I'm worried about the message that it sends to other leaders and to staff when we're missing things or when we forget things. Can I support you on this? Can you recommit to being more focused on these pieces so we can be as effective as possible?"

17

Build and Execute Schoolwide Routines

We were in a school lunchroom with a dean in Milwaukee, observing their systems and providing feedback. At this school, educational assistants (EAs) are supposed to support students during lunch. There were 10 tables in the lunchroom and 10 educational assistants on duty to monitor them. What a perfect ratio!

However, instead of each EA being at one table building relationships, praising students for meeting expectations, and redirecting those who weren't, all 10 of those assistants were doing something else. Five were huddled in a corner. Three had their backs to students and were chatting. Another was at their assigned table but was talking on their phone. The last one was just eating their lunch, disregarding what was going on around them.

Now, this is not how *we* would run a school, but if this was the school's plan, we would discuss them pivoting. Our bigger fear was that expectations in this area didn't even exist. And we were right. The dean shared that none of this stuff had ever been discussed or defined.

Some routines in schools don't directly affect academics but nevertheless have a massive effect on the culture. In that lunchroom, for instance, one student was at an unmonitored table, slamming his tray repeatedly against the wood. There was no one there to address him. Repercussions from such oversights can filter back into the classroom.

Schoolwide Routines

What They Are

These are precise, detailed, and impeccably well-designed and communicated systems and expectations for everything that occurs outside the classroom: arrival, dismissal, lunch, recess, assemblies, fire drills, transitions, and more.

Why They Matter

We should always know what's happening in our schools at all times to the best of our ability. Otherwise, the stuff in our schools that's supposed to be "easy" can wind up becoming really hard. They become distractions that pull time away from instruction—and that pulls time away from making sure that kids are getting the best education possible. Recently, a middle school transition at a partner school took 11 minutes to get 80 students to transition from three rooms to three other rooms. They were yelling, pushing, running, going into rooms that weren't their next room, and running back into their previous room because they "forgot" something while the adults just stood there. That's because there was no routine around it.

Best Practices for Planning

Here's where to start, so dig in.

Name It

With your leadership team, start by naming the places and spaces where these out-of-class routines will be needed. You'll come up with things like arrival, moving to recess, going to and from lunch, and so on.

Define It

With your team, define what you want these to look like from the macro level. What will be the core tenets of any schoolwide routine? Here are some things to focus on: safety, volume, moving with intentionality (but not running), and relationship building (when students are moving from one place to another, it's a great time to share a hello or speak a kind word). Then get into the details. Should the transitions for the little ones require them to walk in lines? Should they be silent? Silent and quiet might as well be one million miles apart, so which is it? When the older students transition, do adults need to be in their doorways? Is leadership present? Since our visit to the school where the transition took 11 minutes, school leaders are there, and now it takes under 3 minutes.

Get impeccably clear about what *everything* should look like and sound like. Do students run out of the building at the end of the day? Likely not. There's probably one area for students who take the bus and one area for kids who walk, take public transportation, or get picked up. There's likely an adult to run lead for each of these groups, dismissing students incrementally, with multiple other adults outside the school to ensure they head out OK.

Best Practices for Staff Rollout

Make these steps a routine part of your work.

Start Early

Set schoolwide expectations over the summer. You may find that things pop up later in the year, and you can attend to those then, but plan to have everything figured out before teachers arrive. This will enable leadership teams to introduce them to teachers, receive feedback, refine, and then practice during the summer.

Introduce schoolwide routines (e.g., fire drill expectations) to students during orientation, assemblies, and the first week of school. For things that are age- or grade-specific (e.g., which stairwells to use for the older students, how to transition in from recess for the little ones), either have one of your leaders demonstrate and allow students to practice during the first week, or have the grade team put together a plan and teach the routine themselves. Commit to teaching expectations as you would teach the curriculum, using lessons, skits, visuals, and modeling to explicitly illustrate expected behaviors in every setting.

Deploy Visual Reminders

Visual reminders help reinforce positive schoolwide routines. Post big ideas like "Please transition silently. Classes are in session" in hallways, restrooms, and common areas and "Have fun, play safely" on the playground. Staff members should refer to them often through shout-outs or any recognitions that celebrate individual students and groups of students who demonstrate expectations.

Safeguard Training Time

Be sure to allow adequate time for professional development, and guard it carefully. Leaders will need to ensure that all staff members understand and use the language, logic, and systems associated with the routines with fidelity. Professional development and reinforcement should occur based on data and trends. Let's say you notice that during fire drills, students are talking and laughing as they're exiting, causing it to take too long. Reset the expectations with the adults, ask them to reset with their students (you can reinforce this at the next assembly), and provide them the language and practice opportunities to redirect talking or laughing students.

Best Practices for Execution

Implementing the following will help ensure a successful execution.

Reinforce and Monitor Routines

Use announcements, classroom meetings, and feedback to regularly reinforce expectations for schoolwide routines for both students and staff. Conduct regular weekly walkthroughs to assess how well people are upholding the expectations for the schoolwide routines.

Take Action

Use the data collected to praise staff and students in places where things look great and to reset in places that aren't as tight as they need to be.

Be Proactive

Reteach expectations after breaks. Remind everyone of the expectations in the weeks leading up to holidays and the end of the year. Work as proactively as possible to ensure that these routines become second nature.

Considerations for Special Education

At the outset, design schoolwide routines with students with disabilities in mind. There should be clearly defined routines for arrival, transitions, instruction, behavior response, and dismissal. These routines should be closely related to schoolwide routines and remain accessible, clearly taught, and aligned with IEP accommodations for relevant students. Predictability and structure significantly improve outcomes for students with diverse learning and behavioral needs (McLeskey et al., 2014; Simonsen et al., 2008).

When changes or adjustments are needed in routines, they should be based on data. We often see routines changed based on feelings or what is best or convenient for adults. Modifications can rely on data such as changes in behavior incidents, time-on-task, and IEP goal progress. Any change to routines must support and not hinder in any way access, inclusion, and learning for the student (McIntosh et al., 2014).

Best practice includes embedding routine execution monitoring during walkthroughs and coaching. Leaders should use shared look-fors to ensure staff consistently implement routines and supports as designed, especially during high-risk moments such as transitions and unstructured times (Fixsen et al., 2005).

Common Pitfalls to Avoid

Be sure to look out for the following pitfalls.

Lack of Clarity and Follow-Through

If you're not crystal clear on your routine expectations, adults will end up enforcing or modeling them inconsistently. Pretty soon, that silent transition could sound like World War III. Also, don't fall into the trap of assuming that students and staff "should know better." A lack of explicit instruction leads to inequity and frustration. To ensure continued credibility, be sure to reinforce or redirect behavior on the spot.

Ignoring Student Voice

If schoolwide routine expectations feel imposed, rather than something they've had some input on, students are more likely to resist them. So while you and your team will create these, asking students how things are going, either informally or formally through surveys, is a great way to increase buy-in. For example, years ago, a school in Los Angeles had teachers walk 6th graders to their next classes. Some students spoke up that it was too babyish, and the school listened. They let them transition on their own to see how they'd do, and they nailed it.

Focusing Only on Negative Behavior

Remember that although you will be looking for places and spaces that aren't yet good enough or meeting the bar, most students and most staff will be doing a great job upholding these schoolwide routines. Make sure to let them know. Thank them. Shout them out.

An Essential Conversation About Building and Executing Schoolwide Routines

Questions to Keep in Mind

- What does "good" look like?
- Are people clear about that?
- Are people meeting that bar?
- Where are the gaps?
- What do I need to address immediately?

The Context: A grade team lead talks to a teacher who is letting 3rd grade students talk and push and run during what should be a quiet, orderly transition.

The Essential Conversation

"Hi, Theresa. Do you have a few minutes? Great. I'm noticing that during your transitions, your kiddos are talking, sometimes loudly, and they're pushing and running as well. I know we both love how energetic our little ones are, but the issue is that it could disrupt other classes. Also, it makes it harder for other teachers to keep their routine expectations sky-high if one person is lowering them. We need you to uphold the expectations we set out at the start of the year. Is that going to be doable for you? Can I support you on this? OK, I look forward to seeing perfect lines starting tomorrow. Thanks very much for hearing me."

18

Evaluate Teacher Performance

We were working with a school in New York a few years back. The school was trying to reconcile the fact that although so many of their teachers were scoring "advanced," "exceeding expectations," or "distinguished" in evaluations, so many of their students struggled. Many of those students were in the 30th percentile or lower in language arts and math, but their teachers were being told, "You're the best there is!"

Now, we're well aware of the myriad factors that lead to strong student outcomes or to the lack thereof. And yes, it's always possible for a teacher to be highly effective while overall student achievement is lower than desired. Sometimes, years of subpar instruction make it hard for even the strongest teachers to close the gap in just one year. Of course, learning differences, home life, and even test anxiety can also negatively affect student scores.

However, we're talking about something different here. We're referring to school leaders who don't routinely observe their teachers and who use rubrics they're barely familiar with to "evaluate" those teachers. It's understandable that this would promote teacher cynicism: "I've hardly seen you all year, and during this random pop-in, you're seriously going to *evaluate* me? I don't even know what's in that framework you're using, and I'm not sure you're any too familiar with it, either."

We believe that in these instances, leaders have an unspoken, wink-wink arrangement with the teacher that sounds like this: "Look, I have no idea what's happening in your room. And I know I'm never in here. So let's do this: I'll write down that you're amazing, and you won't tell anyone that I'm barely around. Because, honestly, I don't even know what to give you feedback on. If I actually did give you critical feedback, you'd most likely push back, and I wouldn't be able to defend any of it."

This unspoken arrangement is pretty common. Average and below-average teachers are being told they're highly effective because their leaders are simply unsure what they're looking for or have no idea what is consistently happening in those classrooms. If the leader does have more clarity there, they often don't want to risk telling teachers how they're actually performing because they know it will cause a blowback that they'd rather not have to deal with. The same thing is happening when it comes to leaders evaluating other leaders. Those rubrics are often even more complex than the rubrics for teacher evaluations, but that rarely matters because almost no one is using them anyway.

This leads to schools where there's so much room for improvement but no one is willing to say it. If someone actually *does* acknowledge the issue, both teachers and leaders—who've always been told they're wonderful, as opposed to being told the truth—push back mightily.

Teacher Evaluation

What It Is

Effective evaluation requires a clear and digestible rubric for teacher performance that leaders and staff thoroughly understand, are trained on, and are normed around. That rubric drives scheduled formal assessments of teacher performance that take place multiple times each year.

(continued)

Why It Matters

In schools, we collect data on student performance all the time. But often, the people who are most charged with influencing student performance—teachers—are left pretty much unaccountable for their own performance. They typically go about their business, getting little formal feedback from leadership.

Evaluations should go well beyond applying to just teachers and academic leads and include people on your operations team, your deans, your administrative staff, the enrollment department, and so on. You may be thinking it's nitpicky or unfair to start evaluating people who've never (or barely) been evaluated before. But the opposite is actually true. It's unfair *not* to evaluate them. They deserve to know how well (or poorly) they're performing based on your agreed-on criteria for success. That formal evaluation will be a part of their record. It should influence their salary, and they should use it as a guide to improve.

Best Practices for Planning

Taking these steps will help you get started.

Create or Decide on the Rubric

The first and most important component to planning for effective evaluations is to have an agreed-on rubric that *everyone* is deeply familiar with. Many schools have a rubric, but few staff members, including the principal, are really knowledgeable about it. They dust it off every few months when it's evaluation time, but they don't use it beyond that. This doesn't work. Moreover, it makes teachers angry to get evaluated on something that no one really understands. Some schools use their rubrics well, but often those are tools they've created, with pieces pulled from multiple sources, which is fine. We recommend the Skyrocket Teacher Evaluation Tool at https://skyrocketed.org/frameworks.

Practice Using the Rubric

Next, have leaders plan and execute lessons, for one another, if need be, that meet the exemplar bar. You need to clearly understand not only the differences among "developing," "proficient," and "advanced" but also what teachers need to do (or not do) to hit each one. This can only happen by planning and modeling lessons that meet those criteria. This should be a fun exercise, because it's also helpful to execute lessons that are done very poorly (and this is where some of the fun might come in) to exaggerate practices that you wish to discourage, practices that are, unfortunately, fairly prevalent in schools—things like not giving clear directions, not introducing an objective at the beginning of the lesson, only calling on the same person because they keep raising their hand, and talking the entire time and not letting students practice.

Decide on Logistics

Finally, determine how many evaluations teachers will receive throughout the year, when they will occur, and who will be conducting them. It likely makes sense, when you kick this off, for multiple members of the leadership team to conduct formal evaluations together. This may make a teacher's blood pressure spike, but in the long term, the norming and collaboration that will occur will make everyone that much better.

Let Teachers Choose

We have one additional tip that we wish we had thought of but that we learned from a partner school. You can make the first evaluation for every teacher *optional* in terms of whether or not it counts. It's the teacher who gets to decide. To lower the temperature and lessen the stress, share this option with teachers before the evaluation. During the debrief, the teacher will decide if they want it to count or not. If they nail it, they'll likely count it. If not, they likely won't.

Best Practices for Staff Rollout

The rollout for an evaluation system or a new evaluation system can be both straightforward and complicated.

Share and Explain the Rubric

There's not a teacher on Earth who doesn't know about evaluations. But they *will* want to know what the rubric is, how it differs from previous evaluation rubrics and processes, whether the evaluation will affect their salaries, whether the evaluations will be announced or not, and so on. Ensure you have answers to all these questions beforehand and share them proactively.

The process is simple in the sense that everyone will know what you're talking about, but it's also complicated because teachers will feel as though you've raised the stakes for them. And so, rightfully, they'll have lots of questions. To be honest, some teachers simply won't like this. That's OK. They need to be evaluated formally. It's how most jobs are run, and teaching should be no different.

If you're already evaluating teachers but, upon reflection, thinking that you don't do it very well, you can take these same steps. Redesign or choose a new rubric or tool, become experts as a leadership team, and then present it to staff.

Model the Rubric for Teachers

The most important component of the rollout is to model for teachers what categories like "developing," "proficient," and "advanced" look like. Almost no one does this, which reinforces the idea that we really don't know what this evaluation thing is all about. It's just something that rears its head a few times a year. A thing we need to endure.

So here's what modeling would look like. To start, clarify that you're going to model something from the tool. Start with something basic, such as classroom routines like entering and exiting, moving from our chairs to the carpet, and handing in homework. Move to more advanced skills (you'll likely need a few sessions for this, and you can always break the school up into content areas with one expert leading each group).

Here's a model for a more advanced skill, questioning techniques, and here's the context: A teacher wants to see what students have retained from the previous day's lesson. Your script might look something like this:

> Let me show you a "minimally effective" questioning technique: "Sam, can you tell me one thing we worked on yesterday?" Now,

> let's look at "effective": "Can I have a volunteer who will tell me one thing we worked on yesterday?" And now, here's a "highly effective" example: "Everyone, please take two minutes to jot down as many things as you can remember from yesterday's lesson. We'll then share with neighbors, and I'll cold-call on a few people to share out."

Of course, that leader would need to ensure they're clarifying what makes these strategies increasingly more effective. But if a leader does what we're describing here, teachers will have a deep understanding of what "good" is, which is so much a part of the evaluation special sauce.

Best Practices for Execution

Ensuring a smooth execution means ensuring that you adhere to the following guidelines.

Be Sure to Capture the Big Picture

Conducting two or three full-period teacher observations over the course of one year is pretty typical. And it's OK. But another model to consider stems from our time at Mastery Charter Schools. Instead of two to three a year, they moved to a model where leadership engaged in five formal observations *every quarter*. These were mini-observations that lasted 15 to 20 minutes. They took place with different classes, during different times of the day, and during different portions of the lessons. They were conducted by different leaders and then combined to lead to *one* score per quarter. This gave leadership a more holistic view of the teaching that was taking place in the school, as opposed to just seeing a single lesson, one that bombed, maybe, or, conversely, one that was stellar but didn't reflect what typically happened in the room.

We've coached leaders to adopt this approach. Although it takes a more intentional approach to planning to make it happen, teachers, in general, prefer it. Also, it further normalizes the idea that the school is a place where getting feedback and having people observing in your room is a part of what you do, which lessens the anxiety that so many teachers feel at "formal time."

Decide: Announced or Unannounced?

Leaders can choose to make these observations announced or unannounced. The latter allows for a more authentic perspective of the teacher's classroom, whereas the former can lead to teachers engaging in more planning than they usually do and even (unfortunately, we've witnessed this) to teachers bribing their students to be on their best behavior so the teacher can score highly.

Both approaches have their advantages and disadvantages. If the visit is announced, maybe it's not such a bad thing for the teacher to engage in extra planning. That might "take" in the long term. Alternatively, if you decide to just pop in one day, you may end up observing students taking an assessment or having a short "brain break."

Considerations for Special Education

Sometimes, because school leaders have taken a hands-off approach to the special ed department, evaluations feel disconnected and hard to execute. The feedback then feels challenging to deliver to teachers who haven't seen the school leader all year. If you have a director of special education and they're the ones evaluating their teachers, that's fine. Just make sure the entire department isn't operating as if day is night, up is down, and that nothing that works in general ed is relevant to them. We say this with love and respect for our special educators, but unfortunately, this happens a lot.

Evaluate your special education teachers. If they need to make significant accommodations for their students (which they may), you should know this in advance. But they should be held to the same rigorous standards as every other instructor in the building.

Common Pitfalls to Avoid

Keep these pitfalls in mind as you engage in this work.

Basing an Evaluation on One or Two Visits

As discussed, it's hard to cherry-pick two lessons out of the hundreds your teachers will teach each year to make a determination about their teaching skill. Realizing that leadership could base half of what they think about you as a teacher on the basis of a single lesson is pretty tough for a teacher. Also, the more you're in a teacher's room, the better they'll feel about whatever their final rating is because they'll realize you have a more realistic sense of their skills. Very few things frustrate teachers more than getting told they're "developing" by someone they're seeing for the first time in their room in January. So, if you *can*, get in there more often.

Failing to Have—or Be Knowledgeable About—a Clear Framework

If you don't have a clear, digestible framework for what good teaching looks like; if you don't ensure you're an expert in it; if you don't ensure that teachers are familiar with it; and if you don't reference the framework often in meetings, email updates, and professional development, then you're pretty much guaranteeing that teachers will push back during and after their formal evaluation debriefs.

An Essential Conversation About Evaluating Teacher Performance

Questions to Keep in Mind

- What does "good" look like?
- Are people clear about that?
- Are people meeting that bar?
- Where are the gaps?
- What do I need to address immediately?

The Context: A principal responds to a teacher who was overheard saying that evaluations don't matter and that administrators don't know what they're doing anyway.

(continued)

The Essential Conversation

"Hey, Mr. Jenkins. Can I share some feedback? Earlier today, I heard you sharing your concerns about evaluations with some other teachers in the lounge. Can I share why we evaluate teachers and why it matters here? Thanks. It's of immense importance that I, as the leader of this building, am continually pushing you all to be your best for students. That happens through coaching, yes, but it also needs to happen in a more formal way as well. My team and I need to be able to see where the wins are and where the gaps are so we can shrink them. We're never able to coach every teacher every year, but we are able to evaluate every teacher every year. Having that record matters for us, but I'd argue it matters for you, too. Knowing where you stand in terms of your performance will only allow you to get better. I don't expect you to love the process after this, but does my rationale make sense?"

Note: This conversation will likely require more input from the teacher. What are their concerns? How can we allay them? But the rationale from you should be similar to what we've written here, so even if the back-and-forth occurs, you'll be armed with it.

19

Set Schoolwide Goals

Antonio recently sat in on a principal's leadership meeting at a middle school in Baltimore. To be honest, the school was in disarray. Teacher morale was low, student discipline referrals were sky-high, and academic performance had been declining for three years straight. The principal was a new leader, and at her first leadership team meeting, she asked a simple question: "What's our goal for this year?"

The room was silent.

One assistant principal finally replied, "Honestly, we're just trying to survive the year."

This happens at schools everywhere, every year. Teams either don't have any goals at all or painstakingly spend time over the summer setting rigorous and meaningful goals around attendance, school culture, teacher retention, academics, and beyond. They put them in a spreadsheet, share them with those who need to know them—and then they never speak of them again. That is, until they get to the end of the year and get a bunch of big surprises (not always bad ones) about where they landed.

This is a huge miss for everyone. Goals direct us; they enable us to gauge progress, to course correct, and to celebrate or recommit when we hit or miss the goals.

That principal realized the problem wasn't just operational—it was cultural. The school had no shared direction. Everyone was working hard, but not necessarily together, and not toward anything clear. So she set bold but focused schoolwide goals: to reduce out-of-school suspensions by 40 percent and increase student attendance by 5 percent by May. She worked with her team to break this down. There would be restorative discipline training for teachers, weekly check-ins with at-risk students, and the implementation of family engagement strategies to address chronic absenteeism. She posted progress trackers in the main office and held monthly data huddles to monitor growth.

For the first time in years, the leadership team united around something specific. They stopped reacting to every crisis and started planning proactively. Teachers began to notice the difference. Students did, too. By the end of the year, out-of-school suspensions had dropped by 47 percent, and daily attendance had risen by 6 percent. More important, the school had found its footing again.

In Antonio's last meeting with the principal, she said, "We didn't get here by chance. We got here because we had goals. Goals don't just measure success. They *create* it." For school leaders, setting clear, measurable goals isn't just a management task—it's a leadership act. Goals align teams, focus energy, and drive the kind of progress that transforms schools.

Goal Setting

What It Is

At its core, goal setting for school leaders is the act of naming what success looks like, putting a stake in the ground, and saying, "This is what we're working toward together and as one team." It's more than just a checkbox on a school improvement plan or a data point in an accountability system. When done well, goal setting becomes the compass that guides every decision, resource, and conversation across a school.

Why It Matters

Goal setting is one of the most powerful tools a school leader has to create clarity, coherence, and accountability in a constantly shifting environment. In schools—where demands are high, where time is limited, and where priorities can easily become fragmented—setting clear, measurable goals provides a necessary anchor for the entire organization.

A well-crafted goal answers the following questions:

- What are we trying to achieve?
- By when?
- How will we know we've made progress?

Imagine a principal at a middle school who notices rising absenteeism and declining reading scores. She doesn't just hope things will improve on their own or through disjointed initiatives and actions. Instead, she sets two clear, measurable goals:

1. Reduce chronic absenteeism by 10 percent by May 1.
2. Increase the number of 6th graders reading at grade level from 45 percent to 65 percent by the spring benchmark.

These goals aren't vague or aspirational. They're precise, time bound, and data driven. More important, they're shared. The principal introduces them to staff, collaborates with teacher leaders to map out action steps, and posts progress dashboards outside the main office. In doing so, that leader transforms a schoolwide problem into a shared mission. Goal setting, then, becomes more than setting a direction. It becomes the backbone of a school's culture of improvement.

Schools are complex systems with dozens of competing priorities. These include academic performance, staff development, student well-being, community engagement, operations, compliance, and more. Without a focused set of goals, leaders and staff risk being pulled in too many different directions. Goal setting narrows the field and focus to help everyone understand *What matters most right now*? This clarity increases efficiency and reduces initiative fatigue.

When goals are shared schoolwide, stemming from the vision and grounded in data, they align the efforts of teachers, support staff, and administrators. Everyone from classroom teachers to cafeteria staff understands how their work contributes to broader outcomes. Sharing clear goals builds a culture of shared responsibility, where progress is not left to chance but pursued intentionally and collaboratively.

In the absence of goals, data are just information. With goals, data become a tool for reflection and action. Setting measurable targets enables leaders to monitor what's working, what's not, and when to pivot. It makes improvement tangible, measurable, and grounded in evidence rather than in assumptions or anecdotes.

Clear goals create fair and transparent benchmarks for evaluating progress. They enable school leaders to hold themselves, their teams, and the organization accountable in a constructive, supportive way. When progress is tracked and communicated openly, it fosters trust and encourages a growth mindset. People are more motivated when they see purpose and progress in their work. Schoolwide goals—especially when broken down into milestones and celebrated along the way—fuel intrinsic motivation. They help staff and students feel the effect of their efforts and see how daily actions contribute to long-term success.

Most important, goal setting forces schools to confront gaps in student achievement, access, or experience. By identifying specific areas for improvement, such as raising literacy rates among English language learners or reducing exclusionary discipline for students of color, schools move from vague intentions to strategic action in service of equity.

In short, *goal setting transforms a school from being busy to being purposeful.* It provides the framework for meaningful progress, keeps the community aligned, and ensures that leadership is not just reactive but visionary and impactful.

Best Practices for Planning

Keep the following best practices in mind.

Align Goals to the School's Vision

Every goal should advance the school's long-term vision and strategic improvement priorities. Remove goals that are not strictly aligned to the vision or consider reprioritizing them.

Use the SMART Framework

Every goal should be specific, measurable, achievable, relevant, and time bound. We didn't create this, but hey, why fix it if it's not broken?

Limit the Number of Goals

Focus on one to three high-leverage schoolwide goals to ensure depth over breadth and avoid initiative overload.

Include Multiple Stakeholders

Invest the time needed to involve teachers, students, families, and support staff in identifying priorities and crafting goals that reflect shared ownership. Do *not* create goals in isolation.

Build in Leading Indicators

Identify short-term benchmarks and mini-goals that signal progress on your journey toward the achievement of your larger goals. You can't simply wait to see the final student attendance numbers at the end of the year. Even for things like state tests, create mock tests that students take multiple times a year. Use those data to inform instruction. Check exit tickets. Look at benchmark assessments.

Best Practices for Staff Rollout

The idea is to keep your goals front and center—at all times and in all places.

Communicate the "Why"

Communicate your goals, and clearly explain their connection to student needs, school priorities, and shared vision and values.

Use Multiple Channels

Reinforce your goals in staff meetings, professional learning communities, newsletters, and visual reminders throughout the school. Everyone in the school community should be able to recite the goals or at least point to where to find them.

Break Down the Goal

Clarify for all stakeholders what success looks like, what actions are required to reach the goals, and how each role contributes to overall success.

Make It Visual

Create posters, goal dashboards, or data walls that make progress tangible and public.

Align the Smaller Work to the Larger Work

Help assistant principals, department heads, and grade-level teams align their everyday work to the schoolwide goals.

Best Practices for Execution

You've laid the groundwork. Now it's time to execute.

Embed Goals in Meetings and Routines

All leadership meetings, professional learning communities, coaching sessions, and classroom walkthroughs should include a discussion that clarifies the progress made on goals.

Monitor Progress Frequently

Use data cycles and progress-monitoring tools (monthly or quarterly) to review metrics, analyze trends, and identify areas that need support.

Celebrate Milestones

Acknowledge individual and team progress with shout-outs, data walls, bulletin boards, and schoolwide updates.

Model Strategic Alignment

Ensure leadership decisions, time allocation, and resource investments reflect the stated goals. If something isn't working, pivot early, with transparency and a commitment to learning.

Considerations for Special Education

Without exception, metrics for success for students with disabilities must be explicitly outlined in schoolwide goals. Ensure those goals address access to grade-level instruction, progress toward IEP goals, and inclusive participation rather than treating special education outcomes as separate or secondary (McLeskey et al., 2014).

Align all schoolwide goals with IEP and MTSS data. For the best outcomes and overall view, use multiple measures (academic, behavioral, and engagement indicators) to ensure goals reflect both compliance and instructional impact for students with disabilities (McLaughlin & Rhim, 2007).

As we've outlined in this chapter, set ambitious, time-bound goals for students with disabilities. The best leaders recognize that high expectations and clearly defined targets are associated with stronger instructional practices and improved student outcomes (Hattie, 2012). This requires you to disaggregate goal-monitoring data by disability status, regularly review trends to identify inequities, and adjust strategies accordingly (Skiba et al., 2016).

And, just in case you missed this point earlier, make goal ownership collective, ensuring leaders, general educators, special educators, and support staff understand how their daily actions contribute to achieving schoolwide goals for students with disabilities (Leithwood et al., 2020).

Common Pitfalls to Avoid

Beware of the following pitfalls.

Setting Vague or Unmeasurable Goals

For example, "We will improve math scores" is not actionable. "We will see a 5 percent increase in middle school math scores as measured by the Illinois Assessment of Readiness" is.

Setting Too Many Priorities

Trying to do it all leads to burnout and to a diluted impact schoolwide and goals that simply go away. In the case of goals and priorities, less is more.

Failing to Revisit the Goal

When goals are not consistently tracked and discussed, they get lost in the shuffle. What gets tracked and measured gets improved—there's no other way.

Opting for the Top-Down Approach

Goals that feel imposed without staff input often lack relevance and negatively affect staff buy-in. Be sure your goals are aligned to what you all care about (vision, values) and represent the voice of your school community.

Celebrating Only Final Outcomes

Focusing only on where you're lagging behind and neglecting incremental wins often lead to early disengagement and low morale.

A Rollout Conversation About Setting Schoolwide Goals

For this chapter, we thought a model of introducing a goal to a leadership team would be most helpful for those leaders looking to do this more intentionally than in the past.

The Context: A principal introduces a schoolwide goal to the leadership team.

The Rollout Conversation

Principal: I want to begin today by grounding us in our shared purpose: ensuring that every student is learning and growing every day. This year, I'm suggesting we set a focused schoolwide goal to help us get there. Based on our spring data, 42 percent of our 4th through 6th graders were reading below grade level. That's not just a number—that's dozens of students who are entering middle school without the literacy tools they need to thrive. Our goal is this: By May, 70 percent of students in grades 4 through 6 will be reading at or above grade level as measured by our end-of-year benchmark. We selected this based on teacher input, assessment data, and alignment with our district's equity plan. It's ambitious, but with focus and collaboration, it's absolutely within reach.

Instructional coach: How will we track progress?

Principal: Great question! Each grade-level team will monitor reading levels monthly. We'll use our professional learning communities to analyze the data, share strategies, and identify students who need interventions. Leadership will support this work by scheduling coaching and providing resources based on what teams need.

Teacher leader: What can we expect in terms of support?

Principal: We're launching a reading intervention pilot, giving dedicated release time for planning, and assigning instructional coaches to work more closely with Tier 2 and Tier 3 supports. But most important, we'll celebrate growth every step of the way—because this is shared work, and we'll get there together.

20

Manage Your Meetings

Recently, we observed a 90-minute leadership team meeting during which only a handful of people spoke. There were zero engagement opportunities, and a number of attendees were busy emailing one another and others in the building.

People have a lot to do, so when meetings don't feel like they matter, people will dread them beforehand, will be resentful during them and work on other things, and will be angry afterward because the meeting wasted their time.

It's easy to blame disengaged employees here, but honestly, it's not their fault. Just like we're more willing to talk or zone out during a movie we don't really like, it's easier to do other things during meetings that meander and feel pointless.

Meetings That Matter

What They Are

These are one-to-one, leadership team, school culture, operations, and all-staff meetings that are engaging, rigorous, and reflective of what the team cares about. These meetings are agenda driven (the agendas are shared in advance), are timed, and are replete with engagement opportunities.

Why They Matter

Effective teams share information and communicate proactively. They set goals, track data, review performance, and share transactional need-to-know information early and often. Meetings are the perfect place to accomplish these things. But they need to be implemented well to ensure they're meaningful.

Best Practices for Planning

Let's consider some actions to take when planning for better meetings.

Consider What, When, and How

You first must determine what meetings need to occur and how often. A principal and assistant principal should hold formal meetings weekly (these leaders would almost certainly connect daily in an informal way). If you're fortunate enough to have a director of school culture, you should meet with them weekly as well. Meetings with someone like the head of enrollment could happen less frequently, perhaps once each month, but maybe more frequently during heavier enrollment months. Leadership team meetings should happen once each week. General staff meetings (not professional development) can happen less frequently, although many partner schools schedule these meetings weekly; sometimes they occur for 15 to 20 minutes before professional development starts.

Here's a list of meetings any leader should be thinking about. You may have more or fewer, depending on your staffing:

- Standup huddles. During these 10 to 15 minutes at the start of each day, leaders share updates on students who may be struggling, staff who are absent and how they'll provide support in those areas, any guests who may be on-site that day, and anything else that feels urgent. These meetings take place in the same space and at the same time every day.

- Leadership team meetings
- Culture team meetings
- Special education meetings
- One-on-one meetings with direct reports
- Grade team meetings. These are usually led by a member of a given grade team to discuss field trips, students of concern, testing, and so on. You should sporadically attend these meetings and provide feedback to the person running them.
- Content team meetings. These are usually led by a member of a specific department to discuss curriculum, lesson plans, students of concern, and so on. Again, attend these sporadically and provide feedback to the person leading the meetings.
- Budget meetings
- Enrollment meetings
- Board meetings. You likely won't schedule these, but they will be on your calendar.
- Meetings with your teacher coaching team. If you have a coaching program, you should meet with the team once or twice each month. You can also ask them to provide updates in leadership team meetings or even turn that portion of the meeting into a general skill-build around coaching.
- Family town halls. Many of our partner schools schedule two to four meetings each year to hear from families. These usually include some light snacks, opening remarks from the leader, and then time for families to ask questions and provide feedback.
- Operations meetings
- Meetings with food services
- Meetings with athletic directors
- Meetings with your manager. Again, you likely won't schedule these, but you will need to account for them.

Schedule the Meetings

Once you've determined which meetings you personally need to attend, schedule these. From our experience, most leaders overschedule themselves. Because they're used to meetings not being very effective or helpful, they think that maybe *more* meetings will get the job done. We believe just the opposite. Have fewer meetings for most things; just make them more meaningful.

Meeting and connecting are good things. Coaching meetings should happen often between leaders and teachers. Stick to those daily huddles. And don't skip leadership team meetings because everyone is "busy."

But meeting with your culture head every day to ask, "How did it go today?" only for them to respond, "Pretty good. We had a few incidents, but nothing we can't handle," is not a great use of time. In this case, meet less and simply expect updates on students of concern and on infractions that rise to the level of suspension or expulsion.

If this level of planning and scheduling is a significant shift for you, be explicit with staff about the change. Otherwise, they might think they're in trouble or that your new interest in attending various meetings is driven by their poor performance. If it isn't a radical shift, however, schedule away.

Align Your Meeting Agendas

Beyond scheduling these meetings, you'll need to create actual skeleton agendas. To the best of your ability, align your meeting agendas so that meeting formats and flow are somewhat uniform from meeting to meeting. We know that this will be impossible to adhere to 100 percent of the time. And of course, a 10-minute standup huddle will usually have a different agenda than a 90-minute leadership team meeting might. Or would it?

Both should begin with some kind of framing from the leader about what they hope to accomplish and then be followed by a check-in with attendees. Then it's on to the heart of the meeting. A leadership team meeting might include some kind of collaboration opportunity, skill build, or brainstorm, which a huddle wouldn't. Still, there'd be a wrap-up with next steps, and then everyone would go on their way. So, although meetings will differ, strive for as much uniformity as possible. It will be more predictable for the team and easier for you to manage across multiple departments.

Figure 20.1 shows a sample agenda for a meeting between a principal and an assistant principal. It's simple and precise, and although we're certain you would need to add to it, given your specific context, using something like this as a foundational component for all meetings will enable those meetings to happen in a much more intentional way.

Figure 20.1

Sample Agenda for a Principal and AP One-on-One

Team Member: Assistant Principal	**Notes:**
Check-in/update: What's one fun thing you did over the break?	
Goal updates:	
Feedback from principal's shadowing (team member reflects first):	
Practice based on feedback:	
Next steps (deadlines, deliverables, etc.):	
Calendar review:	

Best Practices for Staff Rollout

Other than birthday parties (and this is debatable), people generally don't like surprises. Your people are no different.

Share the Shift

If these meetings, their frequency, or these agendas will be a significant shift, your best bet is to gather your leadership team (and others you may wish to include) to share the shift, share the rationale for it, and model a portion of a meeting. This model could be during the intro, the agenda setting, or the practice portion.

The shift will affect team members, so they should get a sense of what the meetings will look like—especially those they'll be involved in—before a given meeting actually occurs. Field questions, ask for feedback, and conclude by ensuring that everyone has a clear understanding of why these meetings are happening, what's going to be different as a result, when their meetings will occur, and what, generally, they will look like.

Share the Rationale

Your people will always want to know *why* something is happening. Anchor the rationale in your realization that you need to provide more direction and support for the team. Anchor it in your belief that *you* can do better at leading them. Anchor it in your commitment to their development and the success of your students. You might say something along these lines:

> Team, I've been reflecting this summer. We had a lot of wins last year. We accomplished X, Y, and Z, for instance. However, as I thought more about the year, I realized that I had left many opportunities on the table where we might have improved. There were times I was unaware of a teacher or student concern; there were times when I was surprised by our lower enrollment numbers; and there were times, quite frankly, when I scheduled pretty boring, transactional meetings that very often didn't even occur because I punted them. This isn't OK. Not for you, our staff, or our students. So I'm committing to being better. I'm going to be

> more in-the-know than I've been before. I'm going to provide more feedback than I have before. I'm going to be more supportive than in years past. And I'm going to ensure that our time together, both as a larger team and individually, is meaningful.

Share what this means—that meetings will be more *intentional* now and will have opportunities for skill development, data sharing, and more tangible next steps. Of course, now you will have to make this come true. People, even your best people, might be feeling some doubt. They may think it means more work, more time, and more commitment from them (which likely will be the case)—and perhaps not all that much follow-through from you (they may doubt your commitment). So say it, execute it, and make it happen.

Best Practices for Execution

Three keys will ensure your meetings go to the next level.

Follow an Agenda

Meetings without agendas meander. They just do. Use an agenda, fill it out, have the team fill it out, or work together to do this, and then share it in advance. Remind people at the start of the meeting what you'll cover. Then stick to it throughout the meeting.

Time Everything

We've all sat through a meeting that's gone on... forever. Thirty-five minutes turned into 50, and then 50 turned into 70, and then 70 turned into 100. Sometimes, there's just too much to cover in one meeting, and this doesn't become apparent until the meeting is almost over. In these instances, leaders should either end the meeting as close to the scheduled end time as possible and save the remaining items for a follow-up, or they can ask specific people to stay longer, if they're able, to finish up.

However, these two options can only work if you were intentional—that is, if you assigned time limits to each portion of the meeting and you stuck to them. The check-in should take five minutes. Each department's data share should take four minutes. And so on. Otherwise, you're running meandering meetings with no end in sight. If the director of operations has eight minutes to talk and then simply keeps on talking *after* the eight-minute alarm on your phone has gone off, you'll accomplish less and anger people more. Time everything: "OK, let's hear from the special education department. You have four minutes to share your data updates. Everyone else, while they're sharing, please write down one thing that resonates with you and one question you have. Go." Be sure to let the speakers know when their time is halfway up.

If this feels cold and unfeeling to you, you might need a perspective shift. Actually, wasting everyone's time and making them late for all their remaining meetings that day—now *that's* the cold and unfeeling thing to do.

Create Engagement Opportunities

The fastest way to get people to check out of meetings is to create conditions that enable them to disengage. When we talk a lot, let a few people dominate the airspace, look at data slides without any calls for action, or ask questions that only a few volunteers respond to, we're letting people off the hook.

When sharing data, do otherwise: "We're going to hear from the culture team. Please take five minutes to share your data updates. Everyone else, while they're sharing, jot down one thing worth celebrating and an area of growth you're hearing. Go." When you, as the leader, have a question, ask everyone to write down a response. For example, "I'm wondering if there's a better way to increase our middle school attendance. Everyone, take two minutes to jot down as many ideas as you can think of. This is a brainstorm, so no ideas are bad. After two minutes, we'll share ideas with neighbors and then share with the whole group."

This *seems* like it will take extra time, but here's the thing: Asking questions to a whole group will usually elicit a handful of responses, ones that are often shared shyly and without a ton of forethought. You'll have fewer ideas, and they simply won't be as good as what we're describing here.

Even one-on-one meetings offer an opportunity to do this. Too often, we'll ask the person meeting with us, "Do you want to practice that, or do you think you're good?" People will *always* say they got it to avoid looking foolish. Ask the person to write down their thoughts: "I just modeled what your conversation with that teacher could sound like. Take five minutes to script your own version. Then we'll role-play it, and I'll give you feedback." It might take more time in the moment, yes, but a whole lot less time cleaning up bungled interactions later.

Considerations for Special Education

As one of our best practices is to engage the entire team during all share-outs, the same should hold true for the special ed department report-out. In fact, pushing them to the front of the line (versus what most teams do, which is to ask them to share last, sometimes running out of time) will reinforce for them and the team that this department matters immensely and that their work is relevant for everyone, not just them.

Common Pitfalls to Avoid

As always, there are some trouble spots to look out for.

Being Unprepared

Sometimes the people running a meeting are so unprepared that it takes the entire meeting just for everyone to collect their thoughts enough to call for a follow-up meeting—on the same topic. To be clear, an intentional meeting to brainstorm and hash out ideas is fine, as long as that's what people know is happening and what they're signing up for. But if it's not, skip the meeting before the meeting by being impeccably well prepared.

Missing Meetings

We get why this happens. You're busy, sometimes too busy to be as prepared as you'd like, so it becomes easier to punt on something that seems to be taking you away from the immediacy of the work. But if you punt too often, team members will begin to feel untethered to your school and your mission. They might even be wondering why they're now meeting after so much time *not* connecting. Leaders are aware of this hesitation (and confusion) from staff; embarrassed, they may tend to punt even more, which can lead to entire teams or departments not meeting for months at a time.

Focusing on the Transactional

Some meetings are way too transactional. They become, basically, a verbal email update. Meetings should include space for skill building, reflection, and work time. When those components are absent, people will wonder why they're meeting instead of just reading an email update.

An Essential Conversation About Managing Your Meetings

Questions to Keep in Mind

- What does "good" look like?
- Are people clear about that?
- Are people meeting that bar?
- Where are the gaps?
- What do I need to address immediately?

The Context: The principal addresses another leader's tardiness for a meeting with a teacher.

The Essential Conversation

"Hey, Mr. Blinken. Can I share some feedback with you? I observed your one-on-one with Ms. Lewis earlier. Both Ms. Lewis and I were at your office promptly at 10:00 a.m. You arrived at 10:08 without acknowledging that you were late. This could send a message to a teacher, in this case, Ms. Lewis, that your time is more important than hers. Now, I am aware that there were several wins in the meeting, so I applaud you for that. But please

(continued)

recommit to starting all meetings on time or communicating that you won't be able to do that and what the new start time is. If you *are* late, please just own it and apologize. I know we have our one-on-one feedback meeting on Friday, but I wanted to get this feedback to you before tomorrow because I know you have back-to-back meetings all day. Can you recommit to this expectation?"

Our Rationale

In this example, Mr. Blinken might be tempted to explain his lateness. And he may have a truly valid excuse, like a five-student fight in the fourth floor stairwell. No one would suggest that this leader should ignore that situation just to keep to the norm of being on time. As people who've broken up more than our share of student fights, we get that the *last* thing anyone is thinking about at a time like that is grabbing their phone to reschedule a meeting.

There's another option, which is simply owning that they were late and apologizing for it. Mr. Blinken could say something like "My apologies for my tardiness. I was handling an issue on the fourth floor. The deans are taking care of it now, but I needed to be there. My apologies again."

Do your best *not* to get bogged down in every little excuse where people can wriggle out of what's expected. This person may have had a valid reason for their miss. But they need to own their misses, regardless of why they occurred.

21

Offer High-Impact Professional Development

When we were teachers, our district brought in some outside professional development facilitators. One in particular stood out. She talked nearly the entire time, gave us zero opportunities to engage with one another, and asked questions in a way that it wasn't entirely clear if she wanted us to respond or if the questions were just rhetorical.

For example, she showed us that well-known David Foster Wallace video about the fish. That's where one fish asks the other fish, "How's the water?" and the other fish, oblivious to the obvious, replies, "What's *water*?" When it was over, she turned to us and said, "Wow. That was powerful, wasn't it?"

When no one raised their hands to contribute, she said, "Oh, come on. *No one* has any thoughts on the video?" At one point, after another "question" like this, Michael called out, in an admittedly obnoxious manner, "Do you want us to answer this? I'm not clear."

The facilitator talked *at* us for three hours. The content was poorly designed and disconnected to what we actually needed as teachers. Very little actually stuck; neither of us, nor anyone we knew, ever used any of the strategies she presented. Ever.

Professional development like that can make teachers cringe. It can make them absolutely *miserable.*

The fact is, professional development is like driving a car—most everyone thinks they're good at it, but they usually aren't. Far too many teachers are figuratively being held hostage by ineffective, boring, and insufficient professional development every year. Teachers show up to crowded classrooms or cavernous auditoriums with little context on why they're there, except for the fact that it's mandatory. They receive little to no data or evidence as to why this "new thing" needs to happen. Instead of being asked to practice the "new thing" in the session, they're simply told to do it later on. Which usually doesn't matter anyway, because no one follows up on the "new thing," so it simply fades away until the next new thing comes along and the cycle repeats itself.

High-Impact Professional Development

What It Is

High-impact professional development is well planned, rich with engagement strategies, and filled with stories and practice. The sessions are relevant because they're piggybacking off a previous session or because the data have shown that the topic is needed. The sessions are delivered in an intentional and precise way by a person who is an actual expert on that topic.

Why It Matters

Teachers don't have the time or bandwidth to sit through stale, stagnant, and, in some cases, unbearable sessions that are irrelevant and presented by someone who's a million miles removed from actual teaching. When done well, professional development can make a real difference for teachers and their students. They all deserve that.

Best Practices for Planning

Start your planning process by considering the following.

Align Professional Development to Schoolwide Goals and Data

Choose topics that address identified gaps in student outcomes, instructional practice, or school culture. Don't just offer one-off sessions. Instead, create a scope and sequence that enables participants to master concepts and build their skills over time. For example, if reading achievement is low, professional development might focus on evidence-based literacy strategies.

Make Sessions Relevant and Actionable

Construct the sessions around relevance, active learning, reflection, and immediate application. Adults learn best when they understand the "why" and can translate things into practical use.

Differentiate by Role and Need

Offer content that's tailored to grade levels, content areas, or leadership roles. Avoid one-size-fits-all training. Nothing is worse than sitting through a training session that is not relevant to your work.

Include Time for Practice and Feedback

Ensure all sessions include modeling, practice, and follow-up opportunities. This is also true for coaching sessions, classroom observations, or professional learning community collaborations.

Engage Stakeholders in Planning

Involve teacher leaders or staff in choosing topics and formats to ensure relevance and increase buy-in. Avoid assuming, in isolation from others, that *you* know what professional development is best throughout the entire year.

Best Practices for Staff Rollout

The rollout process will go more smoothly if you adhere to the following guidelines.

Set Clear Objectives

Clearly communicate what sessions will cover, what participants are expected to learn or be able to do, and how that connects to school priorities.

Build Anticipation and Relevance

Use teaser videos, email previews, or quick polls to spark curiosity and show how professional development can meet real challenges.

Establish Norms for Participation

Set shared expectations around participation, reflection, collaboration, and respect, especially for ongoing or embedded cycles. Some norms we recommend are dive into practice, be tech-free, seek solutions, listen to understand, and be on time.

Leverage Staff Leaders

Share the stage. Use peer facilitators, coaches, or teacher leaders to lead or co-lead sessions, increasing relatability and shared ownership.

Schedule Wisely

Consider the energy levels of participants and their workload. Avoid launching intensive sessions at peak stress times (e.g., during testing season) or when staff members may be distracted by other initiatives or challenges. Also, timing of the year is a factor to consider. Don't roll out something new on December 17 unless you want it to be forgotten by January 3.

Best Practices for Execution

It's crucial to consider the following as you begin the execution phase.

Make It Interactive

Include discussion, modeling, small-group work, and real-time application. Avoid long lectures or passive listening.

Connect to Classroom Practice

Anchor the content in what happens in the classroom. Consider including activities that address student work or that include case studies, lesson plans, or videos of instruction.

Check for Understanding Throughout

Similar to the work we expect teachers to do with students, adult learners can benefit from exit tickets, checks for understanding, peer share-outs, or digital polls to monitor engagement and learning.

Provide Resources and Tools

Provide ready-to-use materials (such as templates, planning guides, and anchor charts) that participants can practice with easily. Be sure the materials are not overly complicated and that their use is appropriate for the time designated.

Solicit Feedback

Gather participant input on usefulness, pacing, and clarity. Ensure that someone from the leadership team follows up with and responds to staff about the feedback. If needed, adjust future sessions accordingly.

Considerations for Special Education

While writing this, we couldn't think of more than a handful of examples, out of hundreds of PD opportunities, where special education leaders or teachers received meaningful training on anything other than compliance. This is a missed opportunity. Whether it's from your director or a third party, your special education team needs development beyond what the entire staff receives.

Design professional development that explicitly builds capacity to serve students with disabilities for all staff. This means prioritizing evidence-based instructional practices, IEP implementation, and inclusive classroom strategies instead of the all too common compliance-only training (McLeskey et al., 2014).

Ensure professional development is job embedded and practice focused. This includes surfacing the shared learning experiences for general and special educators. The hope here is to reinforce the collective responsibility to ensure there is instructional coherence to improve inclusion and reduce fragmentation in service delivery (Klingner et al., 2015).

We cannot overemphasize enough the importance of differentiating professional development with an eye toward role and needs. This is probably the number one piece of feedback we hear. Ensure that leaders, teachers, paraprofessionals, and service providers receive targeted learning aligned to their responsibilities for students with disabilities (Billingsley et al., 2020). Otherwise, you risk eroding trust, commitment, and the overall impact of the learning.

One of the biggest mistakes leaders make is their failure to monitor the impact of professional development. Follow up on the development by using classroom observation data, coaching notes, and student progress toward IEP goals to evaluate whether learning is translating into improved practice and outcomes (Hattie, 2012).

Common Pitfalls to Avoid

Be on the lookout for these common pitfalls.

Holding One-and-Done Workshops

A stand-alone professional development session that lacks a focus on follow-up, ongoing support, or practice will likely be ineffective.

Lack of Relevance

Any professional development must connect to the experience of staff. If it doesn't connect to teachers' real challenges, it leads to disengagement.

Lack of Time to Implement

Staff will need time and space to process and implement what they have learned. Don't rush into a teacher's classroom to observe them implementing a new skill without offering them ample time to practice it. Doing so erodes trust.

An Essential Conversation About High-Impact Professional Development

Questions to Keep in Mind

- What does "good" look like?
- Are people clear about that?
- Are people meeting that bar?
- Where are the gaps?
- What do I need to address immediately?

The Context: This conversation takes place before a scheduled schoolwide session on "Using Formative Assessment to Drive Instruction." Ms. Bryant, the instructional coach, has heard that Ms. Daniels, a teacher, has some reservations about the training.

The Essential Conversation

Ms. Bryant: Hi, Ms. Daniels, thanks for stopping by. I know your time is valuable, and I wanted to check in before our professional development session tomorrow. I heard through the grapevine that you had some concerns about the focus. Want to share what's on your mind?

Ms. Daniels: Honestly, yes. I saw the agenda about formative assessment, and I'm just not sure it's the best use of my time. I've been doing this a long time. I already use exit tickets, checks for understanding, and cold calls. I know what I'm doing when it comes to assessment in the moment.

Ms. Bryant: You've always had a strong grasp of formative checks, your students are consistently responsive, and your pacing is solid.

(continued)

I want to honor that. Can I offer a bit of perspective on why we're still prioritizing this?

Ms. Daniels: Sure. I'm listening, but I just hope it's not the same old stuff.

Ms. Bryant: The goal isn't to reteach the basics. What we're focusing on is how to make formative data more actionable during the lesson—not just collecting the data, but responding to them in real time to make immediate shifts. For example, we're going to look at a few strategies for in-the-moment grouping, adjusting minilessons, and even re-sequencing based on what students are showing us *as* they work.

Ms. Daniels: Hmm. That sounds a bit more advanced than I thought. I usually use my checks to adjust the next day, not always in the moment.

Ms. Bryant: Exactly, and that's where I think you might actually be able to lead. You're strong on the basics, which gives you a foundation to refine and push even further. If you're open to it, I'd love to have you share an example of a strategy that's worked well for you during the session, and then maybe you'll walk away with one or two new moves, too.

Ms. Daniels: So, it's not just, "Here's how to make an exit ticket," but more like, "Here's how to pivot *based* on the data"?

Ms. Bryant: Exactly. And truthfully, you're the kind of teacher I hope speaks up tomorrow, not just for your own growth but for your colleagues who are still building these muscles.

Ms. Daniels: All right, I'll come with an open mind. If it's more about applying in real time, I can see how that might actually help me tighten some things up.

Ms. Bryant: That's all I ask. I'll also send you a quick preview of one of the case studies we're using. You might even recognize the strategy from something I saw in your class last month.

Ms. Daniels: I appreciate that. And thanks for taking the time to talk it through. It makes it easier to walk in tomorrow ready to engage.

Ms. Bryant: Thank you for your honesty. I'll see you in the morning, and I'll save you a good seat!

Closing

Congratulations! You've made it to the end! That's no small feat, considering this book was likely confrontational at times for many of you.

We hope this book has accomplished a few things for you. First, we hope it's reinforced some of the practices you already knew and are doing consistently. We've found that sometimes a leader just needs permission to use data unapologetically or hold people accountable. So ideally, you'll have more freedom engaging in the leadership actions you already engage in—or always knew you *should* engage in.

Second, one of our goals was for this book to speak directly to leaders of urban schools and leaders everywhere who aren't OK with things just being OK, regardless of location. We knew this approach would exclude some people. We also knew that it might lead readers to believe that we think that every last school in every last urban district is an on-fire disaster zone, where nothing good is happening. This is certainly *not* the case. We were OK with these risks, as long as we could honestly speak to what so many of you are feeling: the idea that *you* are the one holding it altogether, the idea that there's very little backup, very little outside support. Hundreds of kids and families depend on you and your team. We know how it feels sometimes. We hope that you feel seen, that you feel more acknowledged after reading this.

Finally, we felt that this book *had* to be written because there are so many of you. When you're in the thick of the work, flipping through this handbook, looking for solutions to the challenges you're facing, know that there's a leader across town, across your state, across the country, or across the globe who's in the same boat. That might not make your work easier, but we hope it's a reminder of how many amazing leaders like you are doing the most important work in education.

References

Ainscow, M., Booth, T., & Dyson, A. (2006). *Improving schools, developing inclusion.* Routledge.

American Society for Training and Development. (2014). *Accountability research summary.* Author.

Archer, A. L., & Hughes, C. A. (2011). *Explicit instruction: Effective and efficient teaching.* Guilford.

Billingsley, B. S., Bettini, E., Mathews, H. M., & McLeskey, J. (2020). Improving working conditions to support special educators' effectiveness: A call for leadership. *Teacher Education and Special Education, 43*(1), 7–27. https://doi.org/10.1177/0888406419880353

Blue-Banning, M., Summers, J. A., Frankland, H. C., Nelson, L. L., & Beegle, G. (2004). Dimensions of family and professional partnerships: Constructive guidelines for collaboration. *Exceptional Children, 70*(2), 167–184. https://doi.org/10.1177/001440290407000203

Carnegie, D. (1981). *How to win friends and influence people.* Simon & Schuster.

Cook, B. G., & Odom, S. L. (2013). Evidence-based practices and implementation science in special education. *Exceptional Children, 79*(3), 135–144. https://doi.org/10.1177/001440291307900201

Darling-Hammond, L., Hyler, M. E., & Gardner, M. (2017). *Effective teacher professional development.* Learning Policy Institute. https://learningpolicyinstitute.org/sites/default/files/product-files/Effective_Teacher_Professional_Development_REPORT.pdf

Fierce, Inc. (2011, May 4). 86 percent of employees cite lack of collaboration for workplace failures. https://www.fierceinc.com/employees-cite-lack-of-collaboration-for-workplace-failures/

Fixsen, D. L., Naoom, S. F., Blase, K. A., Friedman, R. M., & Wallace, F. (2005). *Implementation research: A synthesis of the literature.* University of South Florida; Louis de la Parte Florida Mental Health Institute; National Implementation Research Network.

Fullan, M. (2005). *Leadership & sustainability: System thinkers in action.* Corwin.

Gersten, R., Beckmann, S., Clarke, B., Foegen, A., Marsh, L., Star, J. R., & Witzel, B. (2009). *Assisting students struggling with mathematics: Response to intervention (RtI) for elementary and middle schools* (NCEE 2009-4060). U.S. Department of Education.

Grissom, J. A., Egalite, A. J., & Lindsay, C. A. (2021). *How principals affect students and schools: A systematic synthesis of two decades of research.* Wallace Foundation. http://www.wallacefoundation.org/principalsynthesis.

Grissom, J. A., Loeb, S., & Master, B. (2015). Effective instructional time use for school leaders: Longitudinal evidence from observations of principals. *Educational Researcher, 42*(8), 433–444. https://doi.org/10.3102/0013189X13510020

Hattie, J. (2009). *Visible learning: A synthesis of over 800 meta-analyses relating to achievement.* Routledge.

Hattie, J. (2012). *Visible learning for teachers: Maximizing impact on learning.* Routledge.

Klingner, J. K., Vaughn, S., & Boardman, A. (2015). *Teaching reading comprehension to students with learning difficulties* (2nd ed.). Guilford.

Kotter, J. P. (2012). *Leading change.* Harvard Business Review Press.

Kozleski, E. B., Artiles, A. J., Fletcher, T., & Engelbrecht, P. (2007). Understanding the dialectics of the local and the global in Education for All: A comparative case study. *International Journal of Educational Policy, Research, and Practice, 8*(1), 19–34.

Kraft, M. A., Blazar, D., & Hogan, D. (2018). The effect of teaching coaching on instruction and achievement: A meta-analysis of the causal evidence. *Review of Educational Research, 88*(4), 547–588.

Leithwood, K., Harris, A., & Hopkins, D. (2020). Seven strong claims about successful school leadership revisited. *School Leadership & Management, 40*(1), 5–22. https://doi.org/10.1080/13632434.2019.1596077

Leithwood, K., Louis, K. S., Anderson, S., & Wahlstrom, K. (2004). *How leadership influences student learning.* Wallace Foundation.

Marzano, R. J., Waters, T., & McNulty, B. A. (2005). *School leadership that works: From research to results.* ASCD.

Matthews, G. (2015). *Goal achievement and accountability.* Dominican University of California.

McIntosh, K., Girvan, E. J., Horner, R. H., & Smolkowski, K. (2014). Education not incarceration: A conceptual model for reducing racial and ethnic disproportionality in school discipline. *Journal of Applied Research on Children, 5*(2), Article 4.

McLaughlin, M. J., & Rhim, L. M. (2007). Accountability frameworks and children with disabilities: A test of assumptions about improving public education for all students. *International Journal of Disability, Development and Education, 54*(1), 25–49.

McLeskey, J., Waldron, N. L., Spooner, F., & Algozzine, B. (2014). *Handbook of effective inclusive schools: Research and practice.* Routledge.

Rosenshine, B. (2012). Principles of instruction: Research-based strategies that all teachers should know. *American Educator, 36*(1), 12–19.

Schein, E. H. (2010). *Organizational culture and leadership* (4th ed.). Jossey-Bass.

Senge, P. M. (2006). *The fifth discipline: The art and practice of the learning organization.* Currency.

Simonsen, B., Fairbanks, S., Briesch, A., Myers, D., & Sugai, G. (2008). Evidence-based practices in classroom management. *Education and Treatment of Children, 31*(3), 351–380.

Simonsen, B., Freeman, J., Dooley, K., Maddock, E., Kern, L., & Myers, D. (2017). Effects of targeted professional development on teachers' specific praise rates. *Journal of Positive Behavior Interventions, 19*(1), 37–47.

Skiba, R. J., Arredondo, M. I., & Williams, N. T. (2014). More than a metaphor: The contribution of exclusionary discipline to a school-to-prison pipeline. *Equity & Excellence in Education, 47*(4), 546–564. https://doi.org/10.1080/10665684.2014.958965

Skiba, R. J., Mediratta, K., & Rausch, M. K. (Eds.). (2016). *Inequality in school discipline: Research and practice to reduce disparities.* Springer.

Starner, T. (2015, June 2). Study: Workplace accountability requires a specific strategy. HR Dive. https://www.hrdive.com/news/study-workplace-accountability-requires-a-specific-strategy/400130/

Sugai, G., & Simonsen, B. (2012). *Positive behavioral interventions and supports: History, defining features, and misconceptions.* Center for PBIS & Center for Positive Behavioral Interventions and Supports.

Yoon, K.-S., Duncan, T., Lee, S. W.-Y., Scarloss, B., & Shapley, K. (2021). *Reviewing the evidence on how teacher professional development affects student achievement* (Treatment Summary; REL 2007–No. 033). U.S. Department of Education, Institute of Education Sciences, Regional Educational Laboratory Southwest.

Index

The letter *f* following a page locator denotes a figure.

About the Authors

Michael Sonbert is a bestselling author, speaker, educator, endurance athlete, autism dad, and founder and CEO of Skyrocket Education and Rebel Culture. He's the author of *Skyrocket Your Teacher Coaching: How Every School Leader Can Become a Coaching Superstar* and *Rebel Culture: Build a Badass Team, Drive Results, Become the Ultimate Leadership Weapon*.

Sonbert has turned his passion for educational reform into a global call to action for educational and corporate leadership transformation. He's dedicated the past 20 years to coaching, partnering with, and researching leaders from public schools around the globe to Fortune 500 companies. He's committed to helping leaders grow thriving, impactful, purposeful organizations.

Sonbert's leadership philosophies are currently being taught in a graduate course at the University of Notre Dame's leadership program. Partners include Google, Northwell Health Systems, Oakley, Hormel Foods, Paul Mitchell Education, and hundreds of K–12 schools.

Currently living in New York with his wife and three children, he sits on the board of the autism nonprofit organization, Families for Inclusion.

Dr. M. Antonio Vance is an educator, organizational leader, and scholar with more than 15 years of experience strengthening schools and school systems in the United States and internationally. He currently serves as Chief Schools Officer at Skyrocket Education, where he partners with district and charter leaders to drive instructional improvement, develop leadership capacity, and design systems that advance equity and student success.

Vance has led large-scale school turnarounds and coached executive teams and principals to deliver measurable gains in academic outcomes, school culture, and staff retention. His leadership is grounded in experience as a school leader and science teacher, ensuring his work remains deeply connected to classroom realities.

He holds a doctorate in education from the University of Pennsylvania, where his research focused on whole-child and personalized learning models across international contexts. Vance is also a university instructor, published author, and national speaker on leadership, equity, and school improvement.

About ISTE+ASCD

ISTE+ASCD's mission is to empower educators to reimagine and redesign learning through impactful pedagogy and meaningful technology use. We achieve this by offering transformative professional learning, cultivating and disseminating thought leadership, fostering vibrant communities, and ensuring that digital tools and experiences are accessible and effective.

Related Resources

At the time of publication, the following resources related to this book's topic were available:

The Definitive Guide to Instructional Coaching: Seven Factors for Success by Jim Knight

Embracing MESSY Leadership: How the Experience of 20,000 School Leaders Can Transform You and Your School by Alyssa Gallagher and Rosie Connor

The Instructional Coaching Handbook: 200+ Troubleshooting Strategies for Success by A. Keith Young, Angela Bell Julien, and Tamarra Osborne

The Instructional Leader's Guide to Closing Achievement Gaps: Five Keys for Improving Student Outcomes by Teresa D. Hill

Is My School a Better School Because I Lead It? by Baruti K. Kafele

The Principal's Guide to Conflict Management by Jen Schwanke

The Resilient Rural Leader: Rising to the Challenges of Rural Education by Melissa A. Sadorf

Results Now 2.0: The Untapped Opportunities for Swift, Dramatic Gains in Achievement by Mike Schmoker

The Six Priorities: How to Find the Resources Your School Community Needs by Luis Eladio Torres

Stop Leading, Start Building: Turn Your School into a Success Story with the People and Resources You Already Have by Robyn R. Jackson

Turning High-Poverty Schools into High-Performing Schools, 2nd Edition, by William H. Parrett and Kathleen M. Budge

What If I'm Wrong? and Other Key Questions for Decisive School Leadership by Simon Rodberg

For up-to-date information about ISTE+ASCD resources, go to iste-ascd .org/books. To learn more about membership and join or renew, go to iste-ascd.org/membership, email memsupport@iste-ascd.org, or call 1-800-933-2723 or 703-578-9600.

www.ingramcontent.com/pod-product-compliance
Lightning Source LLC
LaVergne TN
LVHW010054170826
845678LV00012B/2140

* 9 7 8 1 4 1 6 6 3 4 5 0 8 *